THE FIELD GUIDE

FOR

B.A.L.A.N.C.E.

IN A WORLD OF CHAOS

MATTHEW SIMONS

The Field Guide for Balance in a World of Chaos by Matthew Simons

www.fieldguideforbalance.com

Book Design by Chris Adams

Edited by Sara Steinberg

ISBN: 979-8-9863219-0-5

Table of Contents

B

**BREAK OUT
OF YOUR OLD,
LIMITING MINDSET**

L

**LIVE IN THE
MOMENT**

A

**ADJUST YOUR
REACTION**

A

AGAPE

N
NEWTON'S
3RD LAW

E
EASIER THAN
YOU THINK

C
CREATE YOUR
NEW MINDSET

Acknowledgments

Thank you to the obstacles that I faced in life, because I would not be the person I am now without the lessons learned.

A special thanks to my wife Madonna for being a jumpstart during my darkest hours; without her actions, I would not be alive and this field guide would not exist.

This book was originally launched through Kickstarter, so I'm grateful to everyone that was involved in that campaign, and especially want to thank the following supporters, who pledged above and beyond.

Jeromy Dixson

Stephanie Gilfeather

Piper McGee

Hilary Oatfield

Bruce Patin

Jennifer Qui

Bill Sepich

Karen Steepy

Linda Ward

INTRODUCTION

"We are what we repeatedly do. Excellence, then, is not an act, but a habit."

— Aristotle

I used to hate myself, but I kept it hidden from everyone (at least I thought I did). But as my self-hate blossomed, I turned to substance abuse and opiate addiction to numb my pain. Every situation in life seemed like a perfect excuse to self-loathe and remind myself why I was so worthless. Yet on the outside, I appeared happy, joyful, confident, and successful. It was all an act, because on the inside I was dead, pretending to be what I thought the world wanted me to be. I became sick and tired of blaming everyone for why I was miserable. Finally, I realized that the only thing holding me back from finding true balance within myself was me. Everything I was doing was reinforcing the very things I was trying to be free from. The problem wasn't my actions—it was my thoughts and mindset.

THOUGHTS CREATE MINDSET AND MINDSET CREATES REALITY

How often do you think about your thoughts? Probably not much, because you are too busy surviving and fighting to keep your head above water. That disconnection from your thoughts is the reason you feel stuck. Your thoughts aren't just random words swirling around your head; they are the very seeds that help create your attitude toward life and how you walk through this world. If your head is filled with negative thoughts, you can't simply overcome that by pretending to be happy or positive on the outside. You need to change what is feeding the negativity.

Your mindset is so ingrained into your daily operation that you don't even know where it begins or ends (let alone what it looks like), but everything in your life revolves around it. Your mindset is a constantly evolving operating system that is created and molded through every trauma, thought, experience, reaction, and life circumstance. It provides the instructions to your mind and body on how to function in every situation that arises. Everything in life is a byproduct of your mindset, and every solution and action is filtered through your mindset.

Simply put: change your mindset, change your life.

WORK / LIFE BALANCE
+
THINGS
≠
HAPPINESS

If you don't have balance in your mindset, you will never find work/life balance. Most things in your life will ask for more than you can give, so it is up to you to prioritize your balance: emotionally, spiritually, and physically. For many this is difficult, so we turn to objects, substances, or other distractions to give us temporary relief from the pain of existence. The result is a wanting for something you can feel burning from the inside, but you don't know how to extinguish it. I searched for this "something" for years and only found myself frustrated and depressed when I couldn't quench my yearning for it. Maybe if I just collected enough things or experiences I would be happy, so I tried and tried and no matter what I accomplished or purchased or conquered, I still eventually felt hollow inside. Sure, I would have moments of happiness, but they were never sustained.

My initial path to happiness led me to rock bottom, where I was finally able to clearly see that you don't find happiness, you only create it—it is a byproduct of your mindset. That was the exact opposite of what I had been taught, and that was when every aspect of my life began to shift.

Balance, happiness, or any other state of being is a mindset. It is a mindset you have been creating with every thought, trauma, experience, reaction, and circumstance you have ever had. It is a tapestry of every parent, grandparent, guardian, or anybody that spent significant time in your emotional development. Mindset is learned, so the old operating system must be replaced with a new one in order to expect any different results in your life.

Whatever your situation is right now, you are the only one that will able to change it. Finding your balance, adjusting your mindset, transformation, and growth will be uncomfortable at times, and it can be extremely challenging to face the things you have been trying to avoid for years. Self-help stops being fun when it goes from surface level to the deep dive in personal growth. Run toward the emotions, the fears, the pain, and then when you experience them, their illusion of power over you will be gone. Your life will appear messy, but the results will be beautiful. Don't let this be scary, but rather empowering and a call to action. Nobody will save you, nothing will fix you, not even this field guide will help you. You—the person you judge in the mirror every morning—will be the only one that can make any of this happen. Stop giving others the power to dictate your worth in life.

Circumstances, experiences, traumas are only anchors that are used as excuses for not moving through life. I'm not saying pain and suffering are not real. Instead, it is time to no longer let the pain and suffering continue to hold you back and define you; it is time to shift into a new mindset. Don't be hard on yourself—few have been taught this, and even just a couple steps in the right direction will dramatically change your life. It is easy to get stuck in your ways. This is ingrained over years and years of reinforcement, so that eventually, the way you react or get happy or sad feels like it is no longer in your control. Some systems we rely on to help heal are at times outdated and are stuck in old patterns and mindsets themselves. So we assume that this is just how life is going to be. Let me help you: that is incorrect. I only know that because I used to think the same thing. I grew up learning my reactions from those around me, and my family was unconsciously teaching me the same dysfunctional ways of operating as a human being. Not being any wiser, for years I would blame them for not being "better," but they were just playing out the same dysfunction they had learned. I would often be ashamed of my family's actions and reactions. It wasn't until years later that I eventually realized I was doing the same things as an adult that I had been judging in my parents, family, and others.

You will have countless opportunities to reset in life. Sometimes those resets are life-jarring while others seem like a blip on the radar. They are all nonetheless important, but that reset will only work if you create real change and shifts in your mindset. Most don't even know where to begin: I was barely 30 and I had no clue how to break out of the monotony of my life and create the passion and purpose that I was so jealous at seeing in others. It took me 10 years to find out how to create sustained balance in my life. Anyone who has picked up this book is probably not looking to wait 10 years to do the same, so I'm not going to waste your time with a sugarcoated, feel-good, surface-level book.

This field guide is a tool and only a tool—the rest is up to you. You have to do the work and face what is keeping you out of balance. Nobody has the answer except you. It is time to wake up and become conscious of every thought, emotion, and action you have. You are in control of your life and where it is going, much more than you realize. Stop being a passenger in life and get in the driver's seat. There will never be a better time than right now. Tomorrow is too far away and only gives you excuses for procrastination.

INSTRUCTIONS FOR USE

"Life is a balance of holding on and letting go."

— Rumi

From this moment on, you need to reprogram the word balance from a seven-letter noun to a power-packed acronym that can create ground-shaking transformation. Every letter of the word balance becomes a step toward achieving balance and, when used together, a formula for life that has no limits.

B - Break out of your old, limiting mindset

A - Adjust your reaction

L - Live in the moment

A - Agape

N - Newton's 3rd law

C - Create your new mindset

E - Easier than you think

BE READY
TO CHANGE

Every day that you continue living your life without making changes is simply reinforcing the life you are currently living. You have slowly become comfortable being the person you are, but the pain of reality is sinking in. Why do you feel stuck on the hamster wheel? Because you keep doing the same damn things over and over—expecting different results. Replace the word excellence from Aristotle's quote in the Introduction with: mediocrity, survival, happiness, compassion, acceptance, low self-worth, or anything you are searching for or struggling with. Do you believe it? Do you believe that you have that kind of power to create your life? Wake up and stop listening to the zombies in the world that have become disempowered and have mastered living out of balance. You have the power, but it will require breaking out of the habits that have created your reality.

You need to adjust your relationship with change. You need to become comfortable with it: change or transformation is part of the natural cycle. Seasons turn and the leaves fall, but humans tend to resist this because we associate change with fear and are uncomfortable with it. That resistance is what creates a significant portion of the emotional pain we experience.

Transformation is scary; just ask the caterpillar, which must let everything melt away in order to become a butterfly. You, too, will need to let everything that no longer serves you melt away, to make room for whatever will bring you true balance, fulfillment, and happiness. You'll have to alter the way you operate in many aspects of your life. So if you aren't ready to make changes to how you speak, think, and communicate in this world, then don't waste your time reading another word. I thought I was ready for years, but I was too busy making excuses about how others were holding me back or did me wrong. You have to let go of the baggage and pain that you carry around.

And more importantly, you will need to change your entire operating system to eliminate what does not work and add what is missing. For example, when you condemn yourself for past mistakes, you get stuck in the trap of self-judgment. Finding balance should not be another exercise in self-abuse or reinforcing how much you hate yourself or your life. It should be a conscious journey of self-discovery, where you learn to love yourself and forgive yourself.

You will be learning a new language—a new way to communicate with yourself and how you express yourself to the world. Part of the entrapment to your old, limiting mindset is entangled in the way you speak. Just as important is the way you communicate to yourself. There is great power in both our thoughts and spoken words, and some will have to be eliminated altogether to help you find your balance. I can't, I won't, I want, and other limiting words and phrases will just keep you stuck, wanting and waiting.

Another part of the process of finding balance will be removing aspects of your life that no longer align with you and are keeping you out of balance. Many times, humans become codependent to those people, places, or things, so it can be difficult to do that. This is why you constantly feel stuck, because you can't get past something that is blocking you. Also, everything isn't broken; there are aspects of you that are amazing and extraordinary. Not everything needs to be let go of— much does, but deciding which is which will need to be mastered.

Resistance to change is what creates most of our pain. If we didn't understand the changing of seasons, we would think those trees that lost their leaves were dying, but that is the natural cycle. We members of Homo sapiens live within both natural and human cycles, but we resist change or growth and halt our momentum by trying to stop something that doesn't need to be stopped. We have seasons in our lives, ups and downs, but your experience will completely depend on how you react to them and what you attract in your life. What if something needs to fall away to get you from where you are now to where you want to be? Adjust how you view change. Acceptance of change needs to be a foundational part of your mindset to help you transform and find your balance.

You are in control of your life. No one is ever going to give you permission to be happy, balanced, successful, at peace with your life. You have to find that and, like most, you weren't taught where to look, let alone that you have the power to create that. We are all on our own unique path. You must begin trusting yourself, rather than listening to all the disempowered people out there who want you to feel as shitty as they feel about themselves.

You have learned from your parents, who learned from their parents, who learned from theirs. So in many ways, you "are" your ancestors in how you react and deal with life. These habits of the mindset have been passed down from generation to generation, so it will take time to break out of family and societal patterns.

Finding balance doesn't mean your life will never be painful or unfair, or that traumatic events will never occur. What it does mean is that a mindset with balance will give you the ability to bounce back sooner. Shit will happen, but you will recover quicker and not get trapped in an emotional loop and pain cycle.

This is a field guide instead of a book for a reason: because you need to observe your emotions and reactions as they happen "in the field" of life. The best time to grow is when you are out of your comfort zone, so you need to become conscious to your emotions and reactions when they happen, in order to transform. You need to dive into what pisses you off and why. And if you aren't truly honest with yourself, you are only delaying finding your balance. What do you think is unfair? Do people not see you or not value you? Who has hurt you, and do you always go to the same place emotionally when you are hurt? When ____ happens, I react like_____. Look for patterns of circumstances that have happened in your life over and over. There are cycles that will continue to repeat in your life until you bring awareness to this and break out of the mindset that creates them.

STOP COMPARING YOURSELF TO UNREALISTIC EXPECTATIONS

The comparison mindset is one of the meanest and most unfair ways you can operate. To use anyone but yourself as a measurement of who you are or how far you have come will only leave you feeling "less than." Balance will look like different things to different people, so stop comparing your life and progress to others. Everyone is on their own unique life path, so the key is making sure you stay on yours. Sure, your path will have obstacles. But you will have the skills and mindset to navigate your journey and not be stymied by the circumstances that are out of your control.

You are on your own timeline for transformation and have experienced your own sets of challenges in your life. So looking at anybody else and using their life path as a measuring stick for your journey is just setting yourself up for failure. Learning to love and accept yourself begins with stopping the constant unfair comparisons that you have been using to reinforce your negative feelings of self-worth.

Whatever you focus on, you will master it, so be specific. Don't accept mediocrity or you will unconsciously focus on mastering that every day of your life. Don't accept not being happy, because you will master that as well. Master being the best version of yourself, and compare your progress to yesterday's version of yourself only.

GOOD VIBES ONLY?

Your vibration or "vibe" isn't just about faking a positive response to everything—your vibe is the sum total of every thought and feeling you have. It is the thoughts, emotions, and reactions you show the world, and it is also made up of what you are hiding from the world and yourself.

Your vibe is constantly shifting and changing throughout the day. Even if you are a high-vibe person, you won't be positive all the time. It is human to react, but it is counterproductive to minimize—to hide from yourself—the time spent in low-vibe thoughts. Pretending the negative doesn't exist only adds more shame and self-loathing to your mindset. You can't hide from the bad thoughts that live in your head. You may think you are concealing your negative vibe from those around you, but the thoughts in your head have a frequency and vibration that can be felt. This is exactly what happens when someone walks into a room and for some reason, you just are repelled by that person and want nothing more than to create physical distance from them. That is from the vibe they are giving off; it is created from everything they think, say, and do (even the things people think they are hiding).

You can't hide from gravity or Newton's 3rd law (in nonscientific terms, for every action there is an equal and opposite reaction). The same universal laws that govern the very fabric of our existence don't care whether you send out high vibes or low vibes: everything you do comes back to you, good and bad. No thought and action is immune to this. Most humans are completely disconnected from the belief that their thoughts and actions create their reality. So they blindly walk through life as a victim, not realizing they are constantly manifesting and creating the very life they are complaining about.

Finding your balance is just the beginning: it is the key that opens the door to big-time transformation. You can't even begin to chase your real dreams when you are out of balance. No matter your age, background, or religion, mastering your mindset through balance has the ability to shift any aspect of your life that is frozen or broken— even take you to another level of performance you never thought possible. If you continue to blame others or fail to integrate the lessons in life, you are bound to experience them over and over again until you master your mindset. Assigning blame will not prevent your pain; it will only delay it.

STOP TAKING THE BATTERIES OUT OF YOUR SMOKE DETECTOR

Stop lying to yourself and suppressing your emotions with substances, distractions, or anything that is derailing you from actually facing what is holding you back. It is like taking the batteries out of the smoke detector while the alarm is screaming, in order to shut the chaos off. The real cause is the smoke from the house burning down, but it is much easier to take the batteries out than to deal with the actual problem. Sometimes the easiest thing is to just make the noise stop, but the source will still be there and you can't avoid it forever.

So when you are ready to turn the page (both in this book and in your life), you need to make an agreement with yourself that you are ready to find balance and transform into who you are meant to be. It doesn't matter whether you speak it, write it, or feel it: the only thing that matters is that you have to be fed up with your old way of living and make the commitment to change.

This is setting an intention. It will be the first of many— and it is powerful. When you are ready to turn the page (both literally and as a metaphor for changing your life), I want you to say out loud, "I got it!" or feel it in your heart or simply check the box.

☐ I GOT IT!

Now, this isn't how you find your balance, but the process cannot even begin until you set the intention. This is an invitation to yourself to begin, and allow the shifts to come into your reality. You need to be in complete agreement with yourself to find balance and shift your mindset. Otherwise you will continue to sabotage your happiness like you have already been doing for years. So, one more time...tell me you got it.

I GOT IT!

WORLD OF CHAOS

"All great changes are
preceded by chaos."
                – Deepak Chopra

Every person has experienced chaos at some point in their life. For some it is brief, while others allow themselves to dwell in the chaos for days, months, years, or even a lifetime. Many think their suffering is unique, but to each individual, their turmoil is their own worst nightmare that triggers their deepest fears and pains. It doesn't matter whether the chaos is within or whether it is coming from the world around you—when chaos takes over, it can feel almost impossible to function in life or to achieve your dreams.

Yet you have a choice. You may not ever have believed you have a choice, but you do. You can cut through the chaos and find your balance. But this will require you to adjust your reaction to the chaos, and use it for fuel instead of an anchor.

Chaos can look like complete disorder and confusion. (In physics, chaos is the formless matter that is believed to have existed before the creation of the universe.) The word has so much power to create or destroy, depending on how it is used: chaos can mean utter destruction or it can be unlimited possibility. How you view the chaos around you is a choice—and the choice is yours and only yours. Everyone has and will experience chaos, again and again. The choice you need to make is not about eliminating the chaos; it is about reprogramming your mindset to handle it differently.

In early 2011, during the worst business trip ever, I found myself left with two choices: end my life or find a new way to live my life. Frozen with the most overwhelming sensation of giving up, I shut my phone off along with my heart and emotions. Sitting in my hotel room for what could have been the last few hours of my life, I pondered how to divide up the remaining pills I had been addicted to for the last decade. I had thought of suicide hundreds of times prior to this trip, but this time it was different. In my mind, I had convinced myself that life was no longer worth living. It seemed that every situation I experienced was reinforcing the idea that ending my life made the most sense.

I was at a point where all I could see was the negative in my life. I felt that I had let myself down, and more importantly, that I had let my family down. None of this was true, but it was the story I had been telling myself over and over for years. I made myself believe that life was not worth living and that my family would be better off if I was dead.

Ever had a dead battery in your car? What was needed to get everything going again? A jump-start. I had nothing left to motivate myself out of the darkness I was in, but all it took was one spark...one ray of sunshine...just one candle to turn the darkest of places into light. My jump-start came in the form of a knock on my hotel room door, prompted by my wife assertively tracking down my whereabouts.

Jump-starts can come from anywhere—a stranger, a friend, family, a situation, an animal, a song, or even the most seemingly random and unexpected thing. They can even come in the form of a book. That is why I wrote these very words, because not everyone is going to have a person there when they need it most. Jump-starts can be that last chance for someone. This book is a jump-start.

For years I never realized I was in chaos, because all I had known my entire life was some form of chaos:

- I was addicted to opiates (OxyContin and morphine) for over a decade.

- I used to hate myself.

- I have had thoughts and plans of suicide.

- I have been a shitty friend, spouse, and father.

- I have spent time in a mental facility.

- I used to be so angry at the world.

- I was born with a cleft lip that required multiple surgeries and speech therapy. This left me with a sinking feeling every time I looked in the mirror or heard myself speak, until I learned to love and accept myself in my 30s.

- I was raised by a dad who was eventually diagnosed with Asperger's syndrome (Autism Spectrum Disorder as it is now called), and I watched how cruel the world can be to people who are different.

- I watched my mom battle health and mental issues most of her life. The summer going into my senior year of high school, her health took a big decline and she was unable to get off the toilet without assistance. I never spent much more than a few hours away from home; otherwise, she would be stuck in the bathroom. We both were too ashamed to ask for additional help or even discuss the situation.

- I have lost everything.

- I have given up.

- I have not been accepting and have judged others unfairly.

- I have been told I am ugly, fat, and not good enough— and believed it.

- I have seen what depression can do to a body and to a family.

- I have let the insecurities of others dictate my self-worth.

- I have experienced and also provided conditional love and emotional abandonment.

- That list barely covers the chaos I have been through. I may have hidden much of this from the outside world, but internally I was in turmoil close to 95 percent of the time. I used to blame all my past experiences on other people, and that just kept the cycle on repeat. I have been ready to end things, where I could not see the light at the end of the tunnel or find any meaning or purpose in life. I have been through it all and survived, and want to let you know that balance is possible.

My point is that no matter what is going on in your life, it is possible—and never too late—to find balance and shift any aspect of your life. Constantly hiding emotions, frustrations, letdowns, and disappointments will eventually lead you to a dead end. Don't let the chaos take over, no matter how much you think there is. No matter the turmoil in your world, it is possible to create the balance you so badly want. Chaos can either destroy you, or it can be the catalyst and fuel for your balance, growth, and transformation. Choose right now to use the chaos for good.

I know things are tough. There seems to be more lows than highs lately in your life. You have been hurt, traumatized, or made to feel less than. I acknowledge that pain. Shedding those feelings can seem almost impossible, because they can take over your mind and become the focal point of your life.

What recurring negative thought patterns have taken over in your life?

Low (or total lack of) self-worth?

Procrastination?

Suicidal ideations?

Addiction or recovery challenges?

Abandonment issues?

Failures?

Childhood/family traumas?

Conditional love?

Hopelessness?

Lack of motivation?

Overwhelming fear and anxiety?

You just feel stuck?

You're unable to let go of the past?

I have been in every one of those dark places. At times it may not seem like there is a way out, but there is. No matter how bad things get, there is always a path back to balance.

CHAOS TAKES MANY FORMS

The world is in chaos and you don't even have the time to think about it, let alone deal with it. For one thing, your attention span is under attack: you are constantly bombarded with endless interruptions from social media, the 24-hour news cycle, advertising, work/family situations, and all the other trappings that come with modern society.

Moreover, you were set up to fail—the entire marketing machine that is the foundation of consumerism is based on making you feel like you aren't enough. That machine has been pumping you full of misinformation since before you can remember.

Also, values in the modern world have been flipped upside down; the symptoms of this are obvious throughout pop culture and society. It seems that for so many, material objects now take precedence over personal and internal values. Because of that, it has become easy to judge yourself unfairly against others.

For these and many other reasons, finding balance in chaos can seem impossible. So is it any surprise that so like many people, you feel out of balance in today's society and don't know where to turn? I felt the same way, until I discovered how to break out of all the limiting mindsets I had gathered over the years. Before that, I was expecting others to save me and build me up, and when that didn't happen, I always felt let down. I would also project my core traumas and wounds into situations, unfairly putting people in positions of seemingly letting me down, which wasn't actually the case. How can others build you up when they feel just as out of balance? So stop walking around expecting those that are out of balance to help you get in balance.

BREAK THE CYCLE...

Or it will repeat, generation to generation. You are a byproduct of your ancestors, more than you realize. The chaos you are in is partially that of your forebears, because while you may have never personally met your great-great-great grandparents, their actions and inactions are influencing you to this day. Your parents are a product of their parents and surroundings, and their mindset is not too far off from yours. Most of us want to be different from our parents or at least an improved version. But whether or not you want to believe it, you are more similar to your parents than you can even imagine.

Perpetuating any dysfunctional pattern that lives in you or your family will only teach it to future generations. Family cycles are tough to break out of when they have been normalized or kept hidden. Also, it can be painful to see something you have been ignoring or hiding from for years. But you are a teacher, more than you realize. Unless you break out of your limiting mindsets, you will be teaching your children and others that you influence the same, limiting characteristics as a blueprint for living. Will you teach balance and transformation, or will you continue to unconsciously teach the same chaos that currently disrupts your life? Adjusting your mindset and operating system to provide new actions and reactions to previously challenging or triggering events is how you truly break family cycles and generational patterns.

"SORRY DOESN'T CUT IT"

Sorry doesn't cut it was one of my least favorite things I would hear while growing up. Looking back now, I can reflect on that and how I taught that same belief to my kids—until I finally became aware of a family dysfunction that was hiding right in plain sight. It can be a damaging thing to hear as a child that apologizing is not good enough: this makes you feel that no matter what you do, nothing will be good enough, and that's a completely disempowering mindset! That same mindset my parents learned from their parents was unintentionally passed on to me, and then I unintentionally did the same thing to my own children that I hated so much as a kid. Realizations like this are sobering moments, but you have to be conscious to see them—you can't be on autopilot. It can sometimes be quicker and easier to numb the pain than to find balance, but damn, it will be worth it.

Emotionally unable to manage the chaos around me, I became addicted to suppressing my emotions at an early age (actually, this was more from a survival instinct). Because the frustration of reality was too much for me to handle, and I didn't have the tools or skills to confront the emotions that were taking over, I tried to shut them off. I also felt that my emotions were often too much for others to deal with, so I needed to stifle them. It was easier to turn my emotions and reactions off than to cope with them, but there is a price to pay for stuffing away all that pain and sadness—eventually they will erupt.

Initially I would try to occupy my emotions with the "normal" distractions of life. But when that wasn't enough, I turned to substances. When even they weren't enough, only a complete disconnection from life took away the pain—but also any positive emotion. At that point, I was essentially a zombie, and that is a dark and lonely road. My healing only started when the suppression of my emotions stopped, and I could really see what I was hiding from.

IF I HAVE EVERYTHING
I WANT, WHY AM I
STILL UNHAPPY?

Some may seem to have it all but that still isn't enough.
Being out of balance is a problem with your mindset that
"things" and substances won't fix. Stop blaming your
family, parents, childhood, job, partner, "enemies," or any
of your circumstances, and take back inner control. Don't
let the world tell you any different: you are in complete
control of how you experience your life. The only problem
is that you weren't given the tools to tackle the daily grind
of modern life and create balance in your world. Your
mindset is the steering wheel for your emotions, reactions,
health, and even your success or failure. Until you break
out of your old ways of thinking and inject balance into
your mindset, every day you'll continue to feel like you
are stuck on that hamster wheel. There simply aren't
enough things, stuff, money, substances, or distractions
that will fill that void within...what you need is balance.

Your story cannot define you, but it can give you a
starting point for creating your new life. The chaos you
feel is directly proportional to the balance or lack thereof

it in your life. It doesn't matter how you got to this point; all that matters is what you do from this moment on. Day by day, reaction by reaction, decision by decision is how you will change. Every day you have the opportunity to plant seeds of change. So, will you keep doing the same things (expecting different results?) or are you ready to make a change? You have so much more power than you currently believe, and that is a limited mindset that you need to break out of, in order to align with your full potential.

BREAK OUT
OF YOUR OLD,
LIMITING MINDSET

"Reality is created by the mind. We can change our reality by changing our mind."

– Plato

Once you wake up to the simple fact that your mind creates your reality, you will no longer unconsciously let your thoughts, judgments, and other dysfunctional aspects of your mindset run rampant. When you realize the true power of your thoughts, you will never again allow the negative to take over your mindset. Most have been taught that everything is somebody else's fault. But all those little thoughts and judgments you carelessly allow to run around in your head are creating the chaos in your world.

It doesn't matter whether or not you agree with Plato's words—your mind shapes the world around you. You may never have even stopped to think about that, or wonder how that works, but it is happening every second.

To be more specific, your reality is created by your mind, and your mindset is at the core of it all. Your mindset either empowers you or holds you back. Your mindset is so embedded into your every action that it can be difficult to see the forest for the trees. Like the air you breathe (you can't see it or grasp it, but it is performing a vital operating function), your mindset is the bedrock of your life. Where you are at, right now in your life, is a direct result of how your mindset is operating. Nothing in your life will change until you shift your mindset first. You cannot become something you do not believe you are capable of being. Before you can even begin to unravel the limiting mindsets you unknowingly carry around, it is necessary to understand what your mindset even is—how it can hold you back or how it can transform you.

Your mindset is your established set of attitudes. It is what makes you tick. It creates your frame of mind, your mentality, persona, and psyche. It is your character, disposition, and temperament. It is your operating system for life. In short, it is what makes you, you.

Most never give their mindset a second thought, yet it is what is driving the boat. It can be hard to believe, but most people have around 60,000 thoughts per day. The majority of those thoughts are negative and repeat day after day. That leaves little time for positive thoughts and expanding mindsets. So you have to take the negative out and force-feed positivity into your mindset until the positive outweighs the negative.

Everything (and I mean everything) operates under universal laws that dictate cause and effect, even your mindset. Newton's 3rd law plays a much bigger role in your life than you may realize, because everything you do comes back to you, even the thoughts you keep to yourself. Whatever your mindset focuses on, you will bring into your reality. That is why you need to stop blaming anyone else for your circumstances, and start cleaning up your mindset. Make sure you are clear with what you are trying to create in your life. If you constantly complain about how life sucks or you aren't happy, I guarantee how things are going to go with that attitude. It isn't punishment; it is the universal laws giving you exactly what you ask for. Every chapter in this book is an important step in bringing balance to your mindset and using the universal laws to create a new reality.

Everything also has an energy or vibration, even your thoughts. That energy acts like a magnet. Your mindset will align with your recurring thoughts, and the universal laws will, in turn, magnetize situations to you that align with your thoughts and mindset. This is already happening—you are creating and manifesting your life right now. Learn to master your mindset so you are in the driver's seat, creating the new reality you want instead of the one you keep living over and over.

How often do computer firms upgrade their operating systems? Most likely, more often than you upgrade your mindset. Anytime a glitch is found in software, a patch or repair is made, and then every couple of years, an entirely new operating system comes out. Your mindset should be no different—continuous improvements, constantly evolving. Treat your mindset just like new operating software: what works, stays and what doesn't, gets reprogrammed. Don't just skip over this and wait to do it later. Instead, when you become aware of a glitch in your mindset, you need to instantly create the patch and make the repair.

Balance can be so powerful and transformational. Do you think you will come up with long-term success when you are out of balance? What will that business plan, idea, or solution to a problem look like? It will look like a direct reflection of the state of balance or chaos you are in. In effect, the good ideas won't even exist when you are out of balance. Yours will be a lifelong journey to seek and maintain balance, and the amount of time you spend in that place of balance instead of the chaos will be directly related to your overall happiness. Every thought from today plants the seeds of intentions that will become your reality tomorrow. Newton's 3rd law explains how those thoughts can keep you trapped in a cycle, and why it feels like Groundhog Day for so many who are constantly reliving the same hamster wheel life, day after day. The day might look different, but it really is just the same old garbage packaged a little differently.

I CAN'T - I WON'T - I DON'T - I AM NOT

Many of the I's you speak of so frequently are hugely limiting phrases that undermine and impair your mindset. Most don't even realize those words have so much power, so they are spouted out without even considering the damage they can do. Because you think you are just speaking the truth, you are able to justify it in your head. Actually, you are reinforcing a vocabulary and limited mindset that will, in turn, create that reality around you. Shoulda, woulda, coulda are powerful words that will only create more regret and more shoulda, woulda, and coulda in your future.

This is why you have to change every aspect of your communication to yourself and to the world. Replace I can't with I can. This may seem simple, but can be harder to apply in your life than you realize. Most of the time your language and communication are unconsciously reinforcing why you can't do something. Be aware of every "I" you speak into reality—is it limiting or empowering? Don't reinforce what you don't want; instead, focus on and reinforce what you do want. By not changing aspects of your life that is are keeping you down, you are accepting that those things will continue to be part of your current life. Instead, change your words... change your life.

Growing up, most were taught through a series of can'ts, don'ts, and no's, so is it any surprise that your mindset is filled with limiting thoughts that keep you stuck? That foundation of limits was built years ago and you subconsciously carry that attitude into so much of your life without realizing it. You have been hearing the language of limiting mindsets since you were in the womb, so it will take time and effort to break out of that constrained mentality you are trapped in.

Break out of the mindset of comparison—comparison is the root of all evil. The only constructive thing you can compare yourself to is yesterday's version of you. Anything else is an unfair comparison and will leave you feeling less than. Where somebody else is on their journey has nothing to do with your journey. You have no idea where they started or where they are going, so comparison will only create confusion and feelings of inferiority.

Fear of the unknown creates so much confusion and ambivalence in your mindset, making you afraid to let go of what is no longer serving you, and too frozen in fear to take the steps necessary to be the very best version of yourself. Sometimes you just need to keep moving; the answers will reveal themselves all in due time and not always in the ways you expect.

Even work/life balance struggles are a mindset issue. "I'm so busy"…"I don't have time"…"I never get to do anything for myself"…"why do they seem to have everything figured out, but I don't"…"It will never happen for me"…"I don't have the money to ___" are powerful affirmations that people constantly repeat to themselves and, in turn, create that reality in their life whether they like it or not.

Those messages of I can't, I won't have been replaying on a loop your whole life, and will continue to repeat until you change the messages. Nobody else will do it for you or give you permission. Only you can do it.

ADDICTION

Addiction takes the best of you—takes both your potential and your accomplishments—and flushes them down the toilet. Living with addiction is like trying to fill a hole inside you that can't be filled, or trying to put out a fire inside you that can't be extinguished.

Society has done a horrifyingly good job of labeling addicts as deplorable or worthless or simply weak in mind, body, and spirit. So is it any wonder that anyone experiencing addiction will hide it until they can't hide it any longer? There is such a stigma connected to addiction that many people sit on their high horses, judging characteristics of others that also live concealed within themselves.

While most people pretend not to be impacted in any way regarding addiction, there are few who will never know the pain addiction causes. Many people are hiding their addictions in plain sight. Some addictions have even become acceptable, depending on one's socioeconomic class. When that is the case, and a person's addiction is justified in their mind, they often fail to see the full extent of the damage they are causing.

Worldwide, as this is being written, about 240 million

people are dependent on alcohol, more than a billion smoke, and some 15 million use heroin or other injection drugs. Opioid abuse and overdoses are breaking horrifying new records every year. Countless others casually abuse substances or prescription drugs.

People can also be addicted to self-sabotage, or disempowering others, or countless other negative activities. Regardless of the substance or behavior involved, addiction is a futile attempt to fill the hole that is created from unresolved pain, trauma, and other negative experiences.

Before I became an opiate addict, my slow journey toward addiction began as a teenager when, through various substances, I tried to shield myself from the emotional pain of life. Beer came first, then hard alcohol along with some other things sprinkled in. A few years later I shifted to non-narcotic pain pills that were supposedly not addictive, which wasn't the case.

When that wasn't enough, my decade-plus opiate addiction became part of my mindset in my early 20s. My addiction was fueled by a lack of self-worth; I was driven out of necessity to suppress and hide from my emotions. By addicted to opiates, I mean grinding a morphine or OxyContin pill between two spoons, snorting it when

I woke up and then every few hours, until I passed out at night from a combination of prescription drugs and alcohol.

I needed an ever-increasing amount of substances to escape my reality, so I didn't have to deal with the pain of living. Portions of my life were severely out of balance, and I needed a crutch to be able to function and ignore the alarm bells that were going off. For years it seemed like I was able to manage the suppression of my emotions through substances, but warning signs were all around me. Constantly sweating, I was unable to function or sleep without something in my system. My brain was perpetually foggy, and I was emotionally detached from myself and those I cared about.

It was easier to numb that pain than to change my reality, but there is always a breaking point. The last step for me was being introduced to rock-bottom, where I was ready to take my life.

Addiction comes in many forms, but it is always a not-so-silent cry for help. Nobody chooses addiction or dreams of being an addict when they are a kid. Instead, addiction creeps into the mindset through suppression of emotions, low self-worth, trauma, and pain. Inside every addict is a human being who slowly got off track, and chaos began to take over.

It can take years to completely rewire your brain from the trauma of serious addiction. That is why the mindset aspect of recovery is so important when you are working through addiction of any kind. You will be in a constant fistfight with your mindset, as it wants to go back to the negative. But you must not let up. Continually shift back to the good, and strengthen those positive neural pathways.

While many negatives are associated with addiction, you can also shift how you use that word: become addicted to finding your balance, or addicted to living your best life, or addicted to helping empower others. Again, how you use words is a crucial choice. Redefine how you have used previously disempowering words; shift their power and meaning within your mind. There is nothing more powerful than using the word addiction for good instead of negative. Become addicted to being the best version of yourself and mastering your mindset.

What mindsets do you want to break out of? What do you need to remove that keeps on saying you are not worthy? I have had the mindset of an addict and had to construct a new mindset and way of living. Mediocrity is a mindset. Surviving is also a mindset. Blaming others for your circumstances is a mindset. Seeing the negative instead of the positive is a mindset. Giving up is a mindset. Even your self-worth is a mindset.

AUTOPILOT

Most people don't give their mindset any thought, let alone the subconscious aspects that are hidden in the depths of the mindset's operating system. Think of this as operating on autopilot. Your mindset is running the show behind the scenes. It is quietly whispering your view of your self-worth to the world, and subconsciously inviting situations to you that align with that view.

The reality is, adjusting your autopilot correspondingly adjusts your life. So to bring balance and change to characteristics that are on autopilot, you need to bring your awareness to those things you are unconscious to. You need to wake up and become aware of your every thought and action. It can be easier to keep your head in the sand, but that will just keep you stuck. You have to prioritize yourself enough and slow down enough to see what you keep on autopilot.

If there are things you don't like in your life and you haven't been able to shift out of them, that is because you keep the same thoughts streaming on repeat in your head—and thanks to Newton's 3rd law, they keep on happening in your life. Most aspects of your life that keep you out of balance are on autopilot mode. So now is the time to get your inner autopilot to work to your advantage, and replace the less than with a new and improved operating system based on anything is possible.

You might think your mindset is hidden from your awareness. But in reality, your mindset is communicating with you all the time. The voice in your head or that internal monologue that says you are not good enough, or you should quit, or you should wait to act on that idea you had—that is the voice of your mindset. That voice is not always negative; there is usually a positive voice too, but many times the negative is much louder. Quite simply, you need the positive to be louder than the negative.

In our modern world, with distractions coming at you from every angle, it can be very hard to hear what that voice is saying. Many times, it can even be too painful to hear your mindset, so you numb your pain with substances or distract yourself with TV or social media. It is time to put your mindset under a microscope and study your habits.

TAKING INVENTORY OF YOUR PATTERNS

To break out of old and/or limiting mindsets, you must observe your patterns. Look at everything you are doing in your life and analyze your whys. Why am I doing this? Because I have to, or do I want to? What aspects of your life or actions or situations are you satisfied with? Which ones are you disappointed with? What are you mad or frustrated about? Is your inner voice speaking negatively or positively? How do you wish your life could be different? What does happiness look like to you? What about success? It can be sobering to actually dive into your mindset and usually see some good, but also see some very limiting mindsets.

When you are calm and everything is fine, your reactions are also calm and composed. So you need to observe and study when and why you freak out, break down, or get triggered. Then put the balance mindset principles to work. Use this field guide like a white blood cell in your body: attack the viruses of low-vibe thinking and limited mindsets.

Anytime something doesn't go your way or someone lets you down, what story do you start telling yourself?

What are your reactionary stories telling you? Listen to them carefully, because they reveal how you truly feel about yourself. Mine would tell me that my cleft lip made me ugly, or I was fat and poor, or I would never be good enough at anything, or that my entire life would be a struggle. My inner voice was full of shit—it was fear-based and insecure. That is why it feels like Groundhog Day for so many, who are constantly reliving the same frustrations over and over. It is time to change that tune.

Conversations with your inner voice plant the seeds of your reality for your tomorrows. Those seeds of self-worth were planted years ago. But traumatic situations can often keep you frozen, and your limiting mindsets will play out in life over and over, until you make a change. I didn't think I was worthy of unconditional love; I thought I was never good enough. So those limiting mindsets would play out in all aspects of my life, only reinforcing those feelings I was trying to hide from the most.

The voice in your head or that internal monologue can tell you many differing (and even conflicting) things. It might say you aren't good enough, while at other times that same voice will tell you that anything is possible and can be a motivating force for good. Even when I was as negative as anybody could be to oneself, occasionally another voice of love and support would come and inject a positivity and a belief that could not be shook—a feeling that I was meant for something special. When that happens to you, take note of the good, reinforce it, and see where that leads.

Often one positive voice takes over the majority of the time, and you have more control than you think in the matter. In the chaos it can be hard to always hear that voice, but the inner voice is revealing: it is your mindset. That mindset is what is creating most situations in your reality. Change your mindset…change everything.

LIMIT YOUR DISTRACTIONS

So many go to bed with the TV on, or music, or some kind of constant noise in the background. The best way to listen to that voice in your head that is constantly expressing the patterns of your mindset is simple: stop and listen. For some that might seem next to impossible. When I started my journey to balance, the voices in my head were screaming! It was uncomfortable to be with my own thoughts, so I created more and more distractions.

You especially need to listen when you are stressed or frustrated or triggered, because that is when the deep, dark mindset comes out, and it is usually the part that is negative. Listen to the thoughts in your head. It is important to not identify with them, but listen to them: let them flow in one ear and out the other. Just let your inner voice vent, but observe what comes out—that is important. Like a stock exchange electronic ticker banner, my emotions constantly used to scroll through negative thoughts, past experiences, and other reasons to reinforce why I should feel like shit. Listen and you will hear exactly what is going on in the autopilot portion of your mindset. It doesn't lie. You might not like what it says, but you need to know, because that's what is running on autopilot when you are letting it. You need to hear the narrative before you can control the narrative.

Limited mindsets are tied to various aspects of life; they hide in how you think, operate, and communicate.

- *Look at your reactions*: are you usually accepting, or are you unforgiving (sorry is not good enough)?

- *Gratitude*: are you thankful for anything or do you only see the negative?

- *Self-talk*: is it more negative or more positive?

- *Purpose*: what are you doing? For example, why do you work? Is it just to make money, or are you fulfilled as a human being in your career? You must infuse agape or unconditional love into your life with purpose. You need to have things you are passionate about and that give you purpose. Without knowing where you are going, without having goals and dreams, you will just be on autopilot—surviving, but not living.

- *Communication*: how do you speak to others and, internally, to yourself? Is your dialog filled with I need, want, have to, must, please, or instead, is it I am? You must speak what you want to be; otherwise, your language traps you into creating and manifesting realities you don't want. I hope to be or I wish I was will only keep you locked in the hope. This sounds bizarre for so many at first, because you do need to learn essentially a new language, a new way of communicating and expressing yourself. The excuse of I am just being a realist will keep you stuck exactly where you are at.

- Nothing will change until you don't allow limiting thoughts to hide in the dark corners of your mindset. Create a journal or use the next page to list the traits you want to be free from. You will be using your responses later in the Create Your New Mindset chapter, so be thorough, concise, and detailed.

Limiting mindsets I intend to break out of:

_____

_____

_____

_____

_____

_____

_____

_____

_____

_____

_____

_____

_____

_____

_____

_____

_____

_____

Inside your head there is a war going on: constant battling between the duality of the world and your thoughts. So how do you balance the opposites in your mind that go back and forth—for example, the power struggle between happy and sad or success and failure? You can either live in constant fear of the "negative," or you can detach your attention from the thought of failure and instead focus on success, what it will look like and feel like. Devote all your "give a shit" to what you want, not what you are afraid of. And yes, that is so much easier said than done. As your mind is accustomed to take the negative route, you will constantly need to shift back to the positive. You have to be able to look at yourself in the mirror after any situation and ask, did I react to that with negativity or positivity? Your end results will be based on the mindset you were in when solving the situation.

You alone have the power to choose what you focus on, but for years you have trained yourself to focus on the wrong thing out of habit. Break that habit now! When a negative thought enters, think of it as an alarm bell and warning to shift into what you want. Your thoughts come in pairs (opposites like light-dark, up-down, mountain-valley, happy-sad, empowered - disempowered), so treat your thoughts like twins. Think of them as an evil twin and a good twin. Your evil twin is constantly filling your mindset with limits, and the good twin is filling your mindset with possibilities. Which one you listen to is a choice. Both will take you on distinctly different paths, so it is time to prioritize your balance and choose the path that will get you there.

Shift your mindset by choosing where to focus your energy and thoughts. Any idea or emotion or belief you nourish will come to fruition. It simply is what you choose to focus on that magnetizes into your life the situations that reinforce your core beliefs about yourself and the world. You have to create a new mindset and new way of operating; otherwise, nothing will change.

I will never be able to _____

[Fill in the blank with limiting mindset.]

I am _____

[Fill in the blank with new mindset.]

I can't _____

[limiting mindset.]

I will _____

[new mindset.]

I am a failure _____

[limiting mindset.]

I love myself _____

[new mindset.]

I should have _____

[limiting mindset.]

I intend to _____

[new mindset.]

I am helpless_____I am in control

This may seem overly simplified, but it is not. You may think it is easy to shift from the negative, evil twin to the positive, good twin. But for years, you have been practicing and perfecting your response to every action in life—and usually that response goes to the negative. When I started my journey to find balance, I could not even look in the mirror and say "I love myself." Many of you also struggle to say something positive.

You have to break the addiction of feeding yourself limiting phrases. Replace it with a new habit of shifting to an empowering message every time you feel yourself spiraling down. This will require reacting differently to the situations you encounter in life, especially the ones that get you out of balance and take you on that downward spiral. I can't stress this enough—your communication and thoughts are what keep you stuck. There is no other way out of negativity, no way to break out of your old, limiting mindsets, other than to clear your head of negative thoughts and replace them with positive and empowering thoughts.

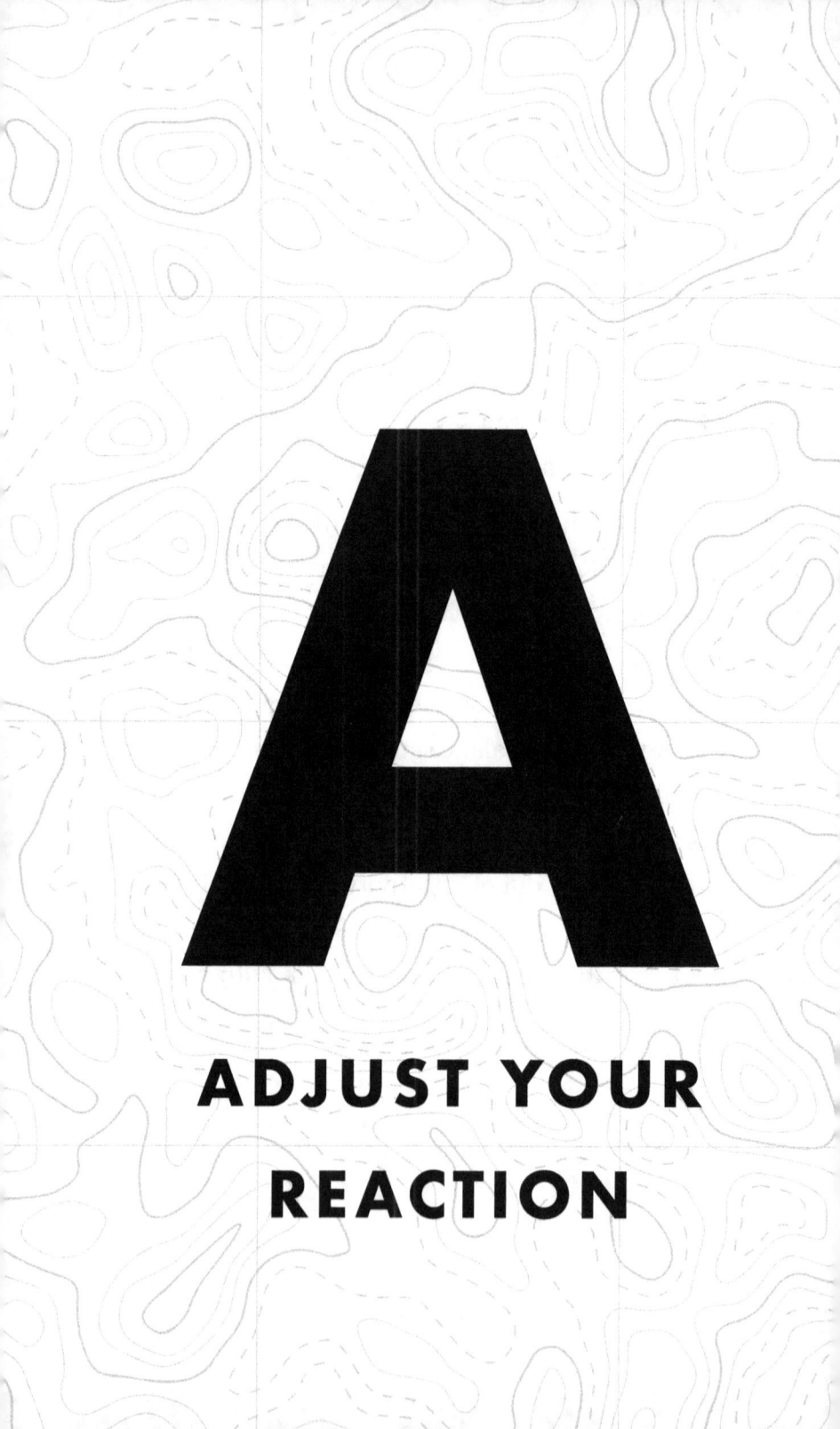

A

ADJUST YOUR REACTION

"You can't change how people treat you or what they say about you. All you can do is change how you react to it."

– Mahatma Gandhi

Every reaction is a glimpse into your self-worth. Paying attention to how you respond when you feel hurt, wronged, or when things don't go your way can give you an objective look into your mindset and subconscious autopilot. It is an opportunity for you to see the good, bad, and ugly in your reactions and the types of responses they trigger. Your reactions are also keeping you in an emotional prison of your own creation, so you have to become aware of what happens and where your mindset goes in order to create a new way of operating.

Most will look at the idea of adjusting their reactions and immediately think they either have little or no control over their reactions, or feel that is just who they are. That is who you are only because you have been training your entire life to become an expert at your specific type of reactions. Each low-vibe reaction drains you; each word or thought involving anger or fear will drain you even if you don't speak it but only think it. Conversely, every high-vibe reaction will lift you up and propel you forward. Every reaction has been a small step toward how you got to this exact place in life. The good news is, you can shift out of where you're at by adjusting your reactions from this point on.

So how will you prioritize yourself? Will you let your emotions continue to drain the energy that you so badly want to save for your dreams, your family, your kids, your spouse, your career? Wasting your energy on low-vibe emotions is a mindset you have become accustomed to, so until you really see this and choose to break free, change will never happen. If you find your gas tank is getting empty quicker and quicker, then you need to look for your emotional drains and also look for opportunities to fill your gas tank back up. There has to be a conscious decision and agreement with yourself to actually begin adjusting your reactions.

PROJECTIONS

Most people are unconsciously walking around with tremendous unrealized emotional pain. Looking for any situation to let others know how bad they feel, they project their core wounds onto every person and every situation they encounter. So if people criticize or treat you poorly, it is a direct reflection of how they feel about themselves, and many times doesn't even have anything to do with you. Yet, so often, most will take all of that pain on and allow it to reinforce negative self-beliefs that live deep within their mindset.

Inserting your pain and trauma from past situations into your everyday current situations is why sometimes small interactions can blow up. Then the usual cycle of feeling less than kicks in. The situation only reinforces the negative stories about your lack of self-worth that you have been telling yourself for years. This is something most people are blind to, but it is creating almost a never-ending cycle of feeling like garbage every single day.

Your reactions will dictate your response. React in fear and you will shift to a mindset of fear, even temporarily. Any resolution or solution in that mindset will be based on low-vibe thoughts and actions and will be rooted in fear.

For example, here's one situation where some of my reactions would be on autopilot. Like clockwork I would start getting "grumpy" on Sunday afternoons, because that meant the workweek was approaching. I never realized I was doing this until my family finally admitted to how my reactions were making them feel. That wasn't even the worst part. Every weekday morning, I would wake up with a sensation of dread in the pit of my stomach, and then instantly feel a wave of anxiety wash across my body. This was my programmed reaction to the workday, and once I noticed it, I realized how much I was draining myself. I was worn out before I even got out of bed, worrying about countless scenarios that could go wrong during the day and all the unexpected items I would have to juggle. Looking back, it is no surprise that my days would end up feeling exactly how I thought they would when I woke up. I was giving away all of my power in almost every situation in my life, and I didn't even realize it.

It is OK to be mad, angry, pissed off as long as you process those emotions in a safe way, and do not either project them onto others, or take them out on others. Suppressing those emotions will only delay the inevitable—having your emotions explode when they are least welcomed.

I speak from experience—I used to just "lose it" about every 3-4 months. The best way to describe this would be an overwhelming feeling of needing to run away into the woods and be alone. You may not think you do this. But anyone who bottles up their emotions is unfairly taking those emotions out on others, whether they realize it or not. Whether you take them out on strangers, friends, or family, it is unfair to those around you. Plus, you are teaching your children and those you influence to continue the same dysfunctional patterns.

DON'T LET OTHER PEOPLE'S JUDGMENTS DEFINE WHO YOU ARE

Listening to the judgments of others can take you to your root pain. Until you face this, you will always give others the power to make you feel like shit.

When others judge you, one or two things are happening:

1. They are judging themselves.

2. If you take offense to their judgment of you, this needs healing within you, somewhere at some level, which requires unconditional personal love and acceptance.

Taking on other people's judgment of you amounts to taking on their pain. Stop the judgment cycle—let them deal with their own life. Being on the receiving end of judgment will not be painful once you understand why others judge: they are only acknowledging how they truly feel about themselves. If you take on any judgments that are thrown at you, then the same pain lives in you both. That really should trigger compassion, but in today's society, it triggers even more judgment. This needs to change, and it either starts with you or the next person that is brave enough to break out of it.

JUDGMENT: USE IT AS A TOOL FOR PERSONAL GROWTH

What you judge in others lives in you in some way, and you will likely experience it at some point in your life. Your unwillingness to see or accept something in yourself makes you judge that in others. Let that sink in for a second: what you judge lives somewhere in you or within your ancestry. This isn't always an apple to apple comparison, so don't immediately dismiss it. Let's say you don't consider yourself a thief, but have you ever stolen someone's trust?

If you examine how you look at judgment, you'll realize it is a powerful tool in finding your balance. Judgment can teach you about who you really are, or it can be a trap that keeps you stuck in patterns and cycles your entire life. Acceptance, which we'll talk about below, is the great neutralizer of judgment. When you view judgment as a tool for personal growth, you will instantly shift your life and eliminate the limits you have been placing on yourself.

Seeing or observing your own limiting beliefs and

mindsets can be challenging. That is where judgment comes in. Your judgments are mirrors that allow you to view aspects of yourself you normally can't see or refuse to see. You can either use judgment as a powerful teacher and tool for self-growth, or use it to keep you trapped in a cycle of self-judgment, which injects mostly less-than and low-vibe feelings into your mindset. When you become triggered by someone else, it is important for you to take note of what emotions and feelings or past experiences are coming up in that situation. Using judgment can be a way to discover your limiting beliefs. Limiting characteristics are much easier to see in other people, so when you do see them in others, remember that they are usually hiding somewhere deep within you.

An even better strategy is to become an observer in life, so replace the word judgment with observation. This doesn't mean you can't study, dissect, or break down something, but the emotional and physical trigger is what comes from your judgment, not from mere observation.

It is easy to say stop judging, but harder to do—years of practice have made you a master of judging yourself and others. So start by shifting how you let judgment work in your life. You may never eliminate the action of judgment, but you can change how you use it. Turn it inward! Understand where judgments live within you; that is where you need to begin with your healing. Once you get to the core of your self-judgments, learning about yourself and where you need to heal, the journey of letting go and healing can begin. What you are judging needs to be healed and released, so let judgment be the teacher that it is trying to be.

What you judge in others, you are unwilling to see in yourself. So you need to not just throw out judgments, but bring conscious thought and reflection to them. Judgment can trigger powerful emotions, so use that power for transformation by aiming those questions toward yourself and away from the other person. Ask yourself, Why am I judging that person? Why am I bothered so much about somebody else's life? What emotions come up when you judge others—fear, frustration, anger? Does what you see in them remind you of anything from your past? How do their life and actions impact you?

You may say BS to the fact that you judge what lives in you, because you think, I'm not a thief; I don't steal. It is safer to judge the thief who has stolen something than it is to judge yourself for robbing your kids of the quality time they deserve from you. Or, who hasn't stolen someone's happiness by striking them down with harsh, unnecessary words? Thieves also steal people's trust. You may think you are so different from what you judge. But if you actually dive past all the surface-level stuff, you will see, in yourself, striking similarities to what you judge in others. Their failings only seem entirely their own because that is how you justify your thoughts and actions in your head.

Think of judgment as identification. Whether good or bad, what you identify in others resides in you, has lived in you, or at some point will live in you. Otherwise your anger, judgment, and frustration would be blind to those characteristics, and you would not waste any time judging them. Pay attention to what you judge, because it will keep on coming up, over and over, in different situations that don't appear connected—but they are. They are trying to bring you to awareness so you can let acceptance tiptoe in and do its job.

Jealousy is another form of judgment. Do you find yourself green with envy when your neighbor, friend, or even a stranger gets some new toy? Jealousy creates a less-than mindset, causing you to repel what you want. Before you can adjust that reaction, you need to understand where your feelings are coming from, no matter what they are. Jealous of someone that seems to have it all? It is a reminder that you are not living your full potential. So take that powerful energy of jealousy, judgment, and anger, flip it into transformational energy, and use it to shift your life. Otherwise a mindset filled with jealousy and anger will only create more of the same. Judgment can be one of the biggest things holding you back, or it can be a powerful tool for transformation when it is used in conjunction with acceptance. The choice is yours.

ACCEPTANCE

Without acceptance, you are pressing the snooze and reset button—you will have to learn a lesson all over again in an even more challenging situation. In order to move forward, you have to accept that everything happens for a reason. That does not mean you have to like what's happening, but you need to accept it. You are also blocking the flow when you don't let acceptance into your mindset. To bring in the new and improved, you have to get rid of the old and limiting.

Judgment and acceptance must work in conjunction. Otherwise you will be stuck in a loop of judgment—acceptance is what breaks you out of that loop. It works like this: Every time you identify and judge a quality in another person, you need to immediately stop and adjust your reactions. What you are identifying in that other person lives within you in some way; you wouldn't react to it or be bothered or upset by it if it wasn't in you. If you can't see it or believe that it could be within you, that is simply because you are ignoring it and choosing not to see it.

Let's imagine that you are judging someone for living a lifestyle you are not comfortable with or disagree with.

I am not saying you have the exact traits of that lifestyle. Perhaps you do, but more importantly, you could be judging the aspect of that person that is speaking their truth or living their life in an aligned way, and not hiding from who they are. Maybe the part of you that doesn't want to see that is the same part of you that feels you are not living your best life and are holding yourself back.

Finding balance and being a master of your mindset takes a lot of conscious thought—to observe, to understand, and to transform—but it is worth it. I imagine a caterpillar is freaked out as its body turns into the goo that transforms into a butterfly. But that short-lived perceived pain is just a shift in its mindset and perception. That degree of transformation may feel like death, but just as with the butterfly, it is a rebirth.

Letting go can be hard! For years I was unable to accept the cards life dealt me, but I was only holding myself back from my full potential. Lack of acceptance keeps you locked in the patterns and cycles you are trying to break free from. That battle in your head oftentimes spills over: you want people to see how much pain you are in, so you lash out at anyone that gives you an opportunity. You and those around you are the ones that pay the price when you are in that mindset, so break out of that low-vibe thinking as soon as possible. Each of my emotional downward spirals would last days or weeks or longer until I could finally snap out of it. Now, for me, it becomes a challenge to see how quickly I can break out of a limiting mindset. So once I become aware, I try to shift as soon as possible after acknowledging it and then accepting it.

Taking back control of your reactions will allow you to take back control of your now. Imagine living each day without stressing about yesterday or what has yet to come. It is powerful. It is transformational. It is called living in the moment—and it is an important characteristic of a balanced mindset.

L

LIVE IN THE
MOMENT

"The secret of health for both the mind and body is not to mourn for the past, worry about the future, or anticipate troubles, but to live in the present moment wisely and earnestly."

– Buddha

Stop time traveling—you are only creating more emotional pain, frustration, and anxiety. What I mean by time traveling is constantly going back in time and reliving a negative experience over and over, or worrying about future events that have not yet happened. The only thing that exists is the now. Your inability to live in the present moment is doing more harm than good.

You may not realize it, but you have become addicted to allowing yourself to feel like garbage. When you go back to situations that have caused pain, that pain can feel just as raw as the day it happened. Emotional pain can be crippling. It can feel as though you were physically punched in the gut! So why are you addicted to constantly going back in time to revisit the emotional aches and traumas of your past? That compulsion is based on your shaky self-worth. Because you haven't actually healed, you are still blaming yourself, and therefore you feel that you are worthy of punishment on a regular basis.

Most people have a daily appointment with their past! It can seem as though the wound is just as fresh as when it first occurred. That doesn't mean at 5 pm you decide to remind yourself how crappy a past situation was. Instead, a pain will resurface in your daily life: Something or somebody will make you feel a certain way. Many times, you will want to blame that person or thing for making you feel that way, but all they did was highlight a pain that already lives within you. Then BOOM! You are transported back to that less than feeling.

You need to be conscious of the situations that are causing you to go back to past emotional trauma. They are giving you a clue about where you need to heal next (it is not about how that person needs to be nicer to you). Only when you accept the root trauma—and that doesn't mean you like it, but you accept it—can you love and forgive yourself. Without that self-love and acceptance, you will be stuck in a holding pattern of constantly reliving your past, and your continued focus on those situations will only manifest more of those situations in your life. You may have been taught that it is OK to constantly beat yourself up emotionally with negative self-talk and revisiting painful situations over and over. But that's what is keeping you out of balance and in an emotional prison where every day, you feel like you are stuck.

This is not just about the past. Constant anxiety and fear of the future similarly sets the wheels in motion through universal laws to attract the very things you are trying most to avoid. There can be no balance in a tug of war! Most people are in a constant tug of war with their emotions, stuck in the past and worried about the future. How do you expect to live in the moment when you are constantly reminding yourself what to worry about? Your fear of the future—driven mostly by your desire to control every aspect of your life—creates enormous stress when things don't line up the way you want or expect them to. Life is meant to be lived, not controlled and feared.

Living in the moment involves accepting yourself right where you are at this very moment. That means changing the way you talk about the present. Stop saying, "In the future I will be happy, balanced, fulfilled or _____ (fill in the blank)." You have to state what you want in the now, like it already exists. That will be difficult at first, but will get easier as you keep practicing. When you say, "I hope to be happy one day," that is all you will create—you will hope to be happy one day (just hope, not the reality). Same goes with your health: if all you do is complain about your body, your body will give you more things to complain about. Your language and communication subconsciously keep you in a prison of your current circumstances.

Instead, you have to be a master of your mindset. Living in the moment is a life-shifting mindset that requires constant adjustments as life throw its punches at you. As long as you are living out of the moment, either worrying about future outcomes out of your control or stuck in the past revisiting old pains, you will forever lose the now:

- One day I will….

- I will be happy when…happens.

- When I retire I will finally be able to do…for myself.

- If…would not have happened, life would be so different or better.

- One day my luck will change.

- The "good" in my life hasn't happened yet, so it never will.

- This is just how things are going to be.

- Why does this always happen to me?

- Life sucks.

- Life is unfair.

- I hate life.

- I will never be able to….

Those are powerful affirmations you are stating, thus preventing yourself from enjoying the now.

So many perceive the daily grind as a negative, but you need to reframe how you view that. The grind is getting you where you need to go, so respect and honor the now, no matter how challenging it is. If you choose to attach positivity and other high-vibe thoughts to the grind, then you will be using the universal laws to your benefit and more positive, high-vibe thoughts will come into your reality. If you reinforce the grind with complaints and negativity, then you will push yourself off course. Instead, focus on empowered and "anything is possible" vocabulary. Then watch whatever situation you are in shift for the good.

What if you have the answers already, but you are in so much chaos by not living in the moment that you have become blind to what is right in front of you or within you? The mindset you are currently in is the capacity from which your solutions will originate. Have you ever tried solving a complicated problem of any kind when you are stressed or anxious? In that situation, you will only come up with solutions from the low-vibe mindset of stress and anxiety. The better your mindset, the better your solutions and outcomes will be.

THE PRESENT
OF BEING PRESENT

Looking back to when I raised my two kids, I can't tell
you how many times that I was not present. I was there
physically, but not consciously. Most often I was on my
phone or computer: working on my endless to-do list,
or worrying—about problems I would face at work
tomorrow, or how life had been so unfair last week, or
fretting about future unknowns. No matter what valid
excuse I had for being mentally absent, I was teaching my
kids, by my example, how to be disconnected from family
and out of balance.

While I may have had a completely different career
than my dad, I was continuing a cycle of false pride by
stating that I was not my dad—whom I had incorrectly
viewed as imperfect due to misunderstanding the root
of his actions. I had been blaming the poor guy for years,
while in reality, I was doing the same exact thing I was
judging my dad for. That was a tough pill to swallow.
But once I acknowledged it, I broke free from any anger
I was holding onto. That is how cycles are broken:
uncomfortable things need to be brought into the light, so
you can see that they are not as scary or paralyzing as you

imagined them to be.

Life only exists in the moment. Fretting about the past? You will only create more of it in the future. You can't learn and enjoy all that life is trying to teach you when you are stuck in time-travelling mode. It is fine to celebrate past victories, but not when looking back is tied to how, for example, you are old and can't do that anymore. All this does is create a low-vibe signal to the world that you want more situations that will remind you how old you are and that you can't do the things you used to. It might seem like I'm saying the same thing, but this is another example of how you have to change your language and communication when you are shifting to a mindset of balance. The "I'm just being honest" justification for looking back at the negative is simply an excuse to reinforce how you are currently feeling. That only keeps you stuck right where you are at. Looking back at the past is fine as a reminder of how awesome you are—as long as it is reinforcing a positive experience with high-vibe thoughts.

Stop holding onto yesterdays with an iron grip. That will only take you off-course and continue to define your future. What kind of power are you giving something that is over? Are all of your yesterdays worth mortgaging all of your tomorrows? Yesterdays can't be changed, but you can change your tomorrow by being present in the now. Adjust to how you look at yesterday and make sure it isn't holding you back from tomorrow.

I'm not saying get rid of your calendar. But rather, adjust your reactions to the things that don't go as planned or become delayed. You don't need to be happy about that, but you need to accept it. There are powers working behind the scenes to align your life with your mindset. So if you judge what the process looks like, you are instantly stopping what you are trying to create or manifest.

That lack of faith in the process is impatience, which is a killer of living in the moment. The stuff that goes through your head when you are impatient could sometimes be borderline funny—if it wasn't so seriously impacting your life. Usually you revisit similar patterns of worry, so what story do you keep telling yourself when impatience and fear kicks in?

Just becoming aware is huge. If you think things are falling apart and believe it, then they will fall apart. Instead, every time that one of your "worry" thoughts appears in your head, you can snuff it out with the opposite high-vibe thought. Be a master of patience: tell yourself and believe, This is working out a different way for a reason. That triggers optimism, which is a higher-vibe thought than fear and concern. Become optimistic and an "anything is possible" mindset kicks in, with high-vibe thoughts focused on expecting the best outcome.

You have to believe that you are on your correct path, even if it doesn't look like it. Your path may be filled with bumps and delays, but that does not mean you should quit when your life gets uncomfortable. Even comparing your current journey to past journeys can potentially derail your progress.

When you constantly look back into the past to create your current identity and how you value yourself, you are pausing your future and missing out on the now. When all of your yesterdays are the sole foundation for your todays, you snuff out creativity and become less and less of who you are meant to blossom into.

It is not denial to avoid talking about negatives. So many people love to dwell on all the negatives that have ever happened. When this makes them feel like garbage, they justify making themselves feel that way because they are "speaking the truth" or "being a realist." That mindset of reinforcing the negatives will only create more negatives in your life. They can be discussed and observed, but do not focus on those feelings. Every time you bring up adverse feelings without resolution, you continue to press the pause button on your healing and balance. There is a fine line between acknowledging and manifesting more of the negative in your life. Only you are in control of that and where you choose to spend your emotional energy. The present is all that exists. Creating any worry, stress, fear, or anxiety is not only holding you back, but it is also holding back anyone else who watches and learns from your actions and words.

PATIENCE DOES NOT MEAN INACTION

Patience doesn't mean you just sit there and let life happen to you—it is the opposite. You need to be moving forward with patience, which is a trust in yourself and that you are on the right path. If you know you are on the right path, then all the turns and curves won't scare you. But without that trust, life will seem frightening, unknown, and almost like punishment at times. Patience is the part of your mindset that lets you enjoy the now and live in the moment.

Don't confuse patience with standing still and waiting for opportunities to magically present themselves. Balance, happiness, satisfaction in life, and even overnight success and amazing once-in-a-lifetime opportunities only align when you are productive and fill your head with positive intentions and beliefs, rather than stuffing it with fear and thoughts of why your intentions won't work out.

Be patient with the intentions you set. The greater the intention, the longer it can take for things to align in order for everything to click. Don't get discouraged that your plans aren't working according to the timeline you set. Remember too that some uncomfortable steps may be necessary. Don't negatively judge the doors that open when they don't lead to your "perfect" vision of what the outcome should be. Sometimes you have to walk through those first doors to get to where you are meant to be. Resisting that walk through that first door could delay or even block all the flow you created and good that was coming your way.

Your life will constantly fall out of balance when you stop participating in it. What happens if you stop participating while driving a vehicle? So why then would you let yourself shift into autopilot and be unconscious to the motivations and mindset you are operating from? A bicycle only functions correctly when you keep moving; otherwise, balance is impossible—humans are no different. Stuff is going to happen that will make you want to collapse and shut down. But you have to keep going, and that requires a mindset that is resilient.

MENTAL TOUGHNESS

There are no tricks or shortcuts to becoming mentally tough. Mastering your mindset and taking back control must become a way of life. This entire field guide is a manual for mental toughness. The exact same steps that will help you find your balance will also sharpen your mental toughness for whatever situations life throws at you.

You can't be mentally tough if you aren't living in the moment; that applies to mental toughness whether on the court, or the athletic field, or in any circumstances of life. When you are living in the moment, you will feel like you are in the zone—where solutions seem to appear out of nowhere, and your mind isn't clouded by chaos. Not living in the moment takes you out of the flow, and your life feels like it has an anchor around it. It is your choice whether to stay in that feeling or to take yourself out of it, based on the situations around you.

When unwanted things happen to you, how much power are you going to give them to ruin the rest of your tomorrows? Don't allow yourself to linger in any thought or situation that makes you feel hindered, suppressed, or small. Have the guts to shift out of it and feel the way you deserve to feel—unafraid and empowered and able to do anything you set your mind to. Become the mentally tough person you are meant to be.

Mental toughness is a mindset that applies to all areas of your life, not just to athletic performance, military service, etc.—it is how you bounce back from anything that hits you in life. Talk to any people who have had any level of success in any industry or profession, and they all will say that at some point, they faced limiting thoughts and felt discouraged, worn out, burnt out, and under enormous stress. Why is it that some will face adversity and continue to take one step at a time, while others will give up and say it is all too much? It is the grit and fight you have. It is the ability to pick yourself up after getting knocked down. It is persevering when you think you should quit. It is staying positive when it's easier to focus on the negative. It is not letting a seemingly insurmountable situation define you.

Having ups and downs doesn't mean you aren't mentally tough. What matters is how much time you spend in negativity, and how quickly you shift out of the past and get back to the present. Mental toughness is about eliminating the draining baggage of limiting thoughts, so you can save your emotional and physical energy for what really matters. Mental toughness calls for focusing on what you have control of and accepting what you don't.

What is critical to putting together a mental toughness strategy is to see your patterns and cycles—your negative tendencies along with the positive ones. Once you know yourself, you will see obstacles coming before they can slow you down. You will be able to shift and adjust.

Being overly and unfairly hard on yourself makes it difficult to bounce back from whatever obstacle you are facing. You need to bring yourself back to balance and ask yourself: are your current thoughts helping or hurting your present situation? You can be your own worst enemy or your biggest cheerleader; it all depends on what you choose to focus on. Focusing on fear and what is not going right only gives away your power and will create more chaos in your mind.

Consciously and with all of your effort, focus on your breath and on what you are able to control. The tougher the situation, the more effort it requires to take back control of your mindset. For years you have trained your mindset to react the exact way you currently do in pressure situations. So from now on, when you're in the midst of pressure situations, you'll need to reprogram your mindset to react differently. Talking about it when you are calm will do nothing. You will have to shift your mindset at times when things are in chaos. That will be tough, but that is how you make real changes to your life. To become a mental toughness warrior, you have to retrain your own mindset.

If you can't let the last play or the last negative experience get out of your head, then you won't be mentally tough or balanced. That sounds pretty obvious, but consider that your self-worth is tied to your mental toughness. So breaking past your own personally defined limits will be a big part of becoming a more mentally tough version of yourself. That requires acceptance and not letting each moment define you on your path to your larger goals.

Once you wake up to how much your self-worth or lack thereof is driving your willingness to give up or continue fighting, you will begin to prioritize finding your balance and loving yourself unconditionally. Loving yourself unconditionally, regardless of the outcome, is easier said than done. So the next chapter is all about helping you do that, through the power of agape.

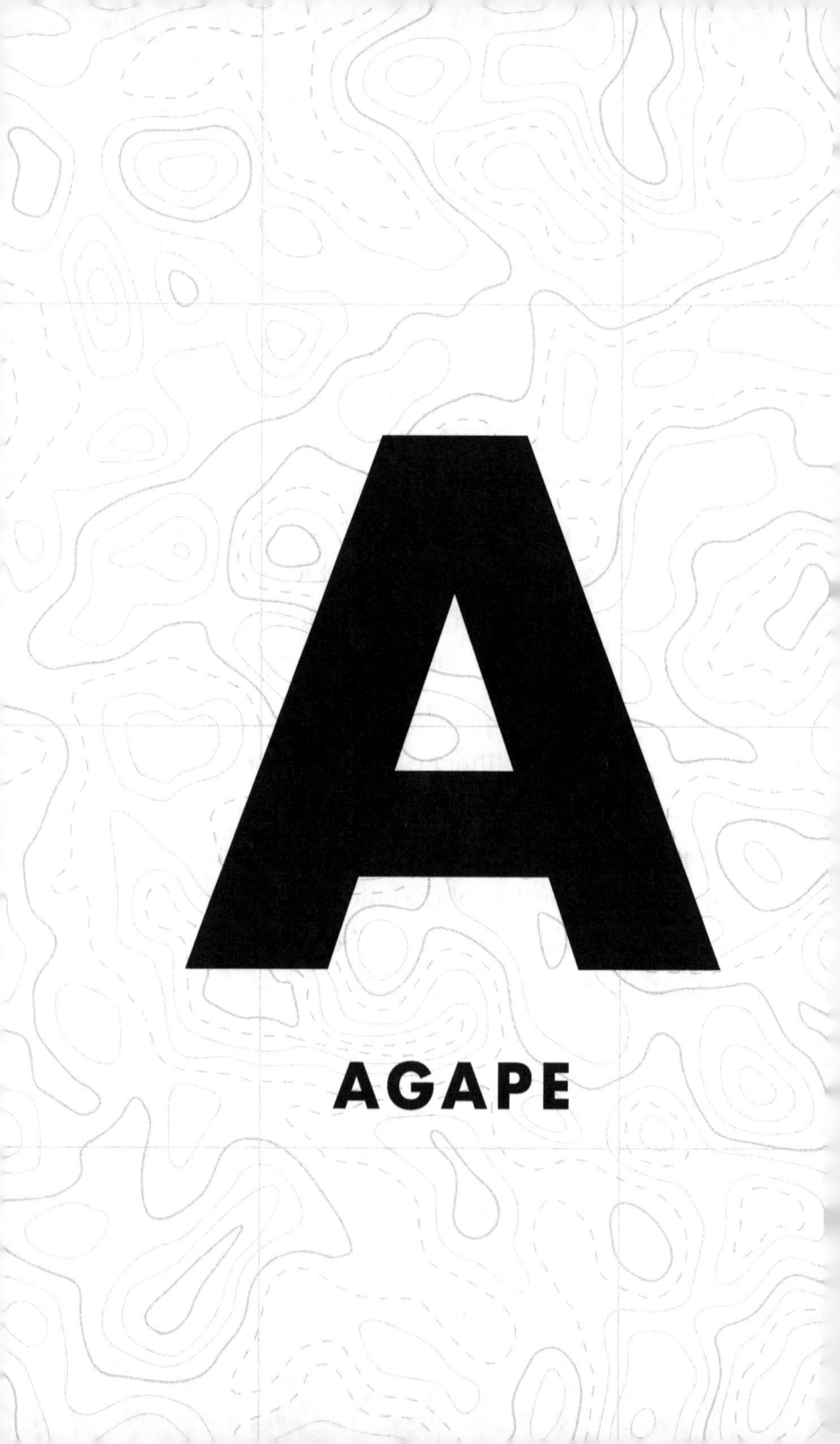

A

AGAPE

"Love yourself first and everything else falls into line." – Lucille Ball

That sounds overly simplified and also a bit like a fairy tale, but it could not be more correct. Love cannot be measured, but we all know it exists. It is the energy that holds life together. Love is usually involved when life is created and also when life ends, but it is the in-between part that most humans struggle with. Love can turn darkness to light but just as easily, light can go to darkness when there is an absence of love or when conditions are put on love.

Everyone has grappled with love in some way. It has long been a source of so much pain and also so much joy. I want to talk about a different kind of love, which will require you to look at love differently and even refer to it with a special word, agape. The love many of us grow up with has conditions tied to it: Love has to be earned; fall in line, otherwise love will be taken away. At times, this conditional love can be the ultimate bargaining chip. But in order for conditional love to exist, there also has to be agape (unconditional love). That means you have a choice. Which love do you want to experience?

The Greeks defined eight types of love; the greatest was agape—selfless and unconditional love. Agape has been described as God's love for mankind. The conditions you put on love are another reflection of your self-worth. Do you believe you are only lovable if you _____ (fill in the blank)? If so, that just reinforces your feelings of low self-worth. Throw the conditions out the window and infuse your life not just with love, but unconditional love. Remember, thanks to Newton's 3rd law, everything you do comes back to you. So if you want more unconditional love or agape in your life, then give it out to the world and watch what comes back to you. It does not work any other way.

Shifting your life from survival mode to long-term balance will be impossible with a closed heart. Pain, letdown, fear, and anxiety have shut down some or all of your heart. The wall you have built around it as a defense mechanism is also keeping you from living your best life. You need to bring more agape into everything you do. Fall in love with life again. Fall in love with your imagination again. Fall in love with your creativity again. Fall in love with yourself unconditionally, and let go of the blame and self-hatred that is weighing you down and holding you back. Focusing on all of your past mistakes will only create more of those situations in your life. Take control of your mindset and inject agape into everything you do. You can't be in a place of hate, blame, or rage when you are in a mindset of agape.

Agape means loving yourself without needing permission to do so. Do the things you love—only those people who are unhappy or don't love themselves will criticize you for living this way. Balanced people, who love themselves and love life, do not attack other people for doing the same. Do you love yourself with agape or do you place the wants of others before yours? Do you prioritize your balance, health, happiness, spirituality? Prioritizing yourself should not be confused with being egotistical or selfish. Instead, prioritizing your overall wellbeing should be viewed for what it is: the foundation and key to finding your balance.

Loving yourself enough unconditionally doesn't mean you will never have a bad day again—it just means that you will not beat yourself up for feeling that way, and you will allow yourself to shift out of it as quickly as you shifted into it. If you are overly sensitive, love yourself for that. If you are too passionate, love yourself for that. If you aren't enough or if you are too much of whatever, love yourself for that.

Love yourself enough to stop comparing yourself to others and using judgment as a tool for self-harm. You need to love yourself, and those who look up to you, enough to break out of your limiting mindsets. You teach by example; most parents eventually learn that their kids will parrot or copy their mannerisms and actions. The best thing you can do for your family is to break the patterns and cycles of your limiting mindsets and reactions, and then watch those traits disappear from your kids and grandkids.

FIND YOUR WHY

Your why is what drives you. It is also your fuel, what keeps you going. Extrinsic motivation can only take you so far. You will never have the heart to give something your all unless you can find the intrinsic motivation from within that will provide unlimited drive and determination. You need to find or re-find the passion you once had for life. You need inspiration and reasons to take that next breath—not because you have to, but because you want to. What have you done for yourself lately? What do you do for self-care? What makes you happy? What is holding you back from getting more of the "happy" in your life? What have you stopped doing that once gave you purpose, or that you used to love doing?

Agape is not living for the acceptance of others, but rather, for complete acceptance of yourself. Embrace your strengths and unconditionally accept the aspects of yourself that others have told you are less than. Stop the negative talk and focus on the good and what you are thankful for. To live in a state of agape or unconditional love is about accepting who you are in this very moment, along with your emotions. There is no upside to judging what you are feeling; you need to allow your emotions and then, if they are negative, shift out of them as soon as you can. Infusing judgment into a situation will just press the reset button, and you will be bound to experience a similar situation again.

Love yourself enough that you no longer live in the shadow of what others tell you is the ideal version of yourself. Instead, break free and trust yourself to be your guide. Plant your seeds of intention for your future, but love yourself enough to not ask permission for the intentions you set and plans you make. When you ask permission to be happy or balanced, no one will ever give it to you. They will give you a million reasons why you shouldn't, or why you are less than, or how difficult it will be, but that is a reflection about how they feel about themselves. The hate people spew is simply a reflection of their pain. You may never have been told that until this moment—but don't listen to that garbage anymore. Doing so will only give it power and take you off your path.

Want to get a real litmus test for how the people around you feel about themselves? Go ahead and talk to people about your wildest dreams, then sit back and observe their reactions. Do they build you up? Or do they tell you why you shouldn't try or how impossible living your dreams will be? Your dreams haven't been created yet, so that is why you mustn't listen to the naysayers. They are reflecting and projecting their negative experience they have not yet accepted, and want to make you feel as crappy as they do.

Many times, you only want to listen to the negative because you are so comfortable dwelling there—so that is all you look for. How many dreams have you squashed and given up on in your life, because others told you they weren't possible? What if, right now, you decided to stop that? Can you even imagine how different your life could look?

Love yourself enough that when you are on your deathbed, you have as few "I should haves" as possible! You were meant to create. Every person is an artist; let your life be your art. Every person has creativity in them; let that express itself in everything you do. You will never regret giving yourself permission to go after whatever creates a spark in your life.

Unconditional love means accepting all of your feelings and emotions. Learn not to judge them, but to accept them. Love yourself enough to adjust your mindset to shift out of those negative feelings, and take back control of the narrative you constantly keep telling yourself.

LET GO OF CONDITIONS

Are you only offering conditional love to the world? To your family? To your kids? To your friends? Do you give love until someone hurts you? Do you only show love if it is given back? Let's take that a step further and replace the word love with acceptance, positivity, encouragement. Do you give out conditional acceptance, positivity, and encouragement? What about loving yourself? How do you expect to unconditionally love others if you don't unconditionally love yourself?

Stop beating yourself up—that ends now. Shift into a new mindset and create the balance you deserve. Love yourself right now and do the same for those around you. When you place conditions on other people, that will create a negative cycle of others putting conditions on you. Everything you do comes back to you! By offering conditional love instead of unconditional love, you will receive back love with conditions. The cycle ends when you stop putting conditions on every aspect of your life.

COMPARISON IS THE ROOT OF ALL EVIL

Comparison can be the root of all evil if you let it. That may seem a little strong. But when the wrong type of comparison kicks in, it opens the doorway to allow dangerous low-vibe thoughts of inferior self-worth to blast into your mindset. The true measure of growth is comparing yourself simply to yesterday's version of yourself. Anything else will take you down a path of feeling (and reacting as) less-than and unworthy.

Society teaches you to compare yourself to unrealistic expectations. For starters, consider advertising. Since the moment advertising first pierced your brain, so many products that generate billions of dollars in revenue have required you to have a low self-esteem and to feel less than. Marketers want you to feel like garbage so you will buy their product. But you are left feeling even more hollow when that object didn't create in you the happiness that was expected. Then disappointment, frustration, failure, feelings of being less than, and other low-vibe thoughts start a dance party in your head. Don't listen to the advertising noise—it doesn't want what is best for you, it only wants your money.

Comparison is infused into your culture, your language, everything you do. That is why it will be a process to break out of the mindset of constantly comparing yourself to someone or something else. Every time that happens, you have to force yourself back to balance and (this bears repeating) compare yourself only to yesterday's version of yourself. Anything else will create a depressed mindset filled with low-vibe ideas. So use discernment and be conscious in all that you do, listen to, and think about.

NO DRAINS

You have countless situations in your day that slowly drain you. One of the worst is anything that triggers you to feel less than. That is one of the most emotionally draining things you can do to yourself. It has got to stop—you are not less than and you never have been. Anyone who tells you anything other than that is simply reflecting onto you how they feel about themselves. Are you surrounding yourself with a higher percentage of people operating with conditional love, or with unconditional love? People who don't love themselves will certainly not show you love. Instead, they will unconsciously try to make you feel just like they do, which is less than and out of balance. Stop allowing others to dictate how you view yourself.

Another of the biggest drains is worry—about the future, or about current situations that are out of your control, or any of the myriad of topics you love to wrap in anxiety. Anything that gives you a bad feeling in the pit of your stomach or makes you feel disempowered or less than will drain you. You know it and can feel it when it is happening, but you need to have enough mental toughness to not accept it any longer. You have to shift that mindset of worry to a high-vibe mindset.

When you are in any negative mindset, it can be hard to get out of it. Saying something positive can feel impossible, and just thinking something positive can seem unimaginable. But if you don't push through, you will get more of what you don't want.

So wake up to the drains you are allowing, and start loving yourself enough to stop giving away your power and life force. Instead of the distractions you waste most of it on, you need to save it for the important things you want to accomplish.

G.A.S. TANK—IS IT FULL?

What do I mean by G.A.S tank, or as I prefer to call it, your "Give a Shit" tank? In every situation in life, you are fueled by how much you care or "give a shit." It is your stamina regarding effort level and your willingness to persevere through obstacles. Some people are filled with "give a shit," but little follow-through. Other people have little "give a shit" and a ton of follow-through.

You are in control of the size of your G.A.S. tank and can expand it if you need to. You are also in control of how you use your G.A.S. If you waste it on low-vibe situations that are out of your control, or by judging or other emotional drains, then you will not have the reserves for when you really need it.

Whenever you have little to no "give a shit" in a situation, then you will get back exactly that. This is a question I constantly ask anyone I coach: Is your G.A.S. tank full or empty? That is an opportunity to truly reflect and become conscious of how you are feeling physically, mentally, and emotionally. It is a check-in with yourself—then and only then can you be aware of how full or empty is your tank. Every day will not be the same. How much the situations of your day drain you, and how well you take care of your personal balance, will depend on how full your G.A.S. tank is.

This can't be faked. What do you really give a shit about; what is important to you? Can you even answer that clearly and concisely? When you stop giving a shit in life, it shows! The only cure is finding passion and purpose in life and in everything you do. You can't be in balance and not give a shit.

Have you stopped giving a shit in one aspect of your life? If so, that is the early-warning sign of not giving a shit in more areas of your life—until you are a big pile of shit: not caring about yourself or others; just trying to survive and get yours. Again, you can't be in balance and not give a shit! So find your purpose...find your passion. I guarantee it will fit into your life, and the shit that doesn't belong will find a way of disappearing.

Remember, your mindset is a reflection of your self-worth. If you can't love yourself unconditionally, then you will subconsciously draw situations into your reality to reinforce those feelings of negative self-worth. On the other hand, just the simple action of agape, loving yourself unconditionally, will attract situations into your life that reinforce unconditional love. Then, just as Lucille Ball said, ...everything else falls into line. The only thing

I would add to that would be: because Newton's 3rd law makes it so.

NEWTON'S
3RD LAW

"If you want to find the secrets of the universe, think in terms of energy, frequency, and vibration."
— Nikola Tesla

The truth has been hidden right in front of humanity for ages, sprinkled throughout metaphors and traditions from nearly all religions and cultures, along with writings and stories from nearly every generation's greatest minds. But few truly listen and even fewer master how to use the truth. Years turn to decades, which turn to centuries, and by now the cancer of disempowerment, causing you to believe your thoughts and actions really don't matter, has become a disease of the world. But people are starting to wake up and take back control of their lives. More importantly, you are starting to wake up to your power; otherwise you never would be reading or listening to these words.

Everything you do, say, or think comes back to you in some way:

You reap what you sow.

What goes around, comes around.

Do unto others as you would have them do unto you (or any other version of the Golden Rule).

Those are not just metaphors, sayings, or verses. Their power is backed up by Newton's 3rd law, which states (for our purposes, in the most nonscientific terms) that for every action, there is an equal and opposite reaction. You can't escape or avoid Newton's 3rd law, but you can learn to work with it to create your best life.

Every thought, whether it is spoken or kept silent in your head, is a seed of intention planted in the garden of your mindset. What grows in the garden of your mindset will eventually come to fruition in your reality. That is a lot of responsibility, because anything you set your mind to, unconsciously or not, will eventually become part of your reality and life experience in some way. This is why becoming conscious of every thought, emotion, and action is so critical. Every moment, you are giving away your power when you don't realize or believe there is a repercussion to operating with a negative mindset. Whenever you sow mental seeds of self-hate or unworthiness, just because you say the words silently in your head does not mean that those thoughts are not creating a ripple effect in the universe and aligning you with exactly what you are thinking about

Everyone emits a frequency like a radio station, and the "songs" it plays are based on your vibration or vibe. Every thought, emotion, feeling, and action has a vibration and frequency. You are constantly and unknowingly broadcasting your song or message or vibe or whatever you want to call it. This is your own, unique, universal signature.

Why is this crucial to realize? Like a magnet, your vibe attracts situations into your life to align with the message from your broadcast. All of the negativity, anger, resentment, and pain you think you are hiding are drawing more of it into your life—and will do so until you change the song to something different.

I didn't say finding balance would be easy, but it will be worth it. Turn your autopilot off as much as possible and try to be aware of what songs, messages, and vibes you are broadcasting. They are a sum total of everything you have swirling in that head of yours, including the things you are trying to hide. Hidden or not, either way this is happening, so you might as well master it.

Newton's 3rd law could care less what you send out—your world will simply respond to it. If you don't take back control from that voice in your head and find balance in your mindset, you will continue to attract the same chaos that constantly seems to visit your life. So stop being unconscious. Wake up to this. Use it to your advantage, instead of letting it keep you trapped in the loop of your current situation.

Let's take a deeper look at the reality of Tesla's quote. According to Albert Einstein, everything in life is a vibration. That means everything is alive with an energy of its own. So why would your thoughts be any different? They aren't: 24 hours a day, 7 days a week, even when you are sleeping, you are subconsciously broadcasting your "vibe" or vibration to the world. Every single thought, even if it is never spoken, is acting like a super-magnet, attracting to you the very situations you dwell on. Every thought, emotion, and action (even the food you eat) will create your own, unique vibrational frequency.

This is why you may come across someone and something just feels off; you want to get away as fast as you can from that person. There can also be people that you are drawn to, almost as if magnetized by their energy. In both situations, often your brain kicks in and tries to overthink the situation. But the truth is, your "antenna" or intuition picked up on something in their vibration and frequency, just like tuning in a radio station. Also as with a radio station, you have the power to tune into whatever you desire. So when you are listening to garbage, remember that is a choice: change the station and the message and vibe will instantly change.

The less you live in the moment, the more you create the situations you are trying to avoid. That requires acceptance to pull you out of not being present. Acceptance doesn't mean you like your current reality, but it does mean you can stop manifesting situations that remind you of your pain and trauma. Many don't want to believe that they are in control, because why would someone want to seemingly punish themselves over and over? That happens because most people are unaware of how healing works. You can't keep suppressing trauma and pain with quick fixes or temporary solutions from money-grubbing industries. Instead, you need to become a mindset warrior and break out of the prison that your mind has created in order to survive the pain of living.

There is nothing you do, or even think, that doesn't involve an even energetic exchange. Everything will be balanced out one way or another, and you can't escape that. There is a cause and effect to everything you do. Steal and you will be stolen from. Lie and you will be lied to. There is no "getting away with" anything in life. You may think you are hiding from the repercussions of your actions and thoughts, but there must be an equal energetic exchange or an equal and opposite reaction, due to Newton's 3rd law. There may be a delay in the outcome of the law of cause & effect, but it will catch up to you at some point (and sometimes in a way you least expect). Years can go by and you may forget who you once were, but your past thoughts and actions still live within you, waiting for you to wake up.

Your Now is designing your future with every thought

and directive from your mindset. If you constantly remind yourself of all the pain you experienced in your past, you will plant seeds of intention for a similar future. If you worry about a potential negative future, you are planting seeds of intention for what you fear most. So be present and live in the moment, in order to manifest a clear and much more direct path to your dreams.

THE LAW OF CAUSE & EFFECT

The universe and everything in it (including you, of course) operates according to at least a dozen interconnected universal laws. The law of cause & effect is one of those. It governs the world such that every cause must have an effect. Since there can be a delay between the cause and effect, most people are blind to how they are intertwined and connected. But if you analyze all of the seeds of intention you have been planting and fertilizing over the years in your mindset (and programming as your "radio station" frequencies), you will clearly see that you are the creator of the good and bad for the majority of situations in your life.

Once the light switch turns on and clarity comes into your mind, that is not a time to beat yourself up for not knowing this sooner. Instead, it is an invitation to begin living life with a new set of eyes and rules such that you are in control. This will necessitate changing many habits, patterns, and mindsets that you have been reinforcing for years. To start building a new path to balance and happiness requires creating an entirely new mindset to operate from.

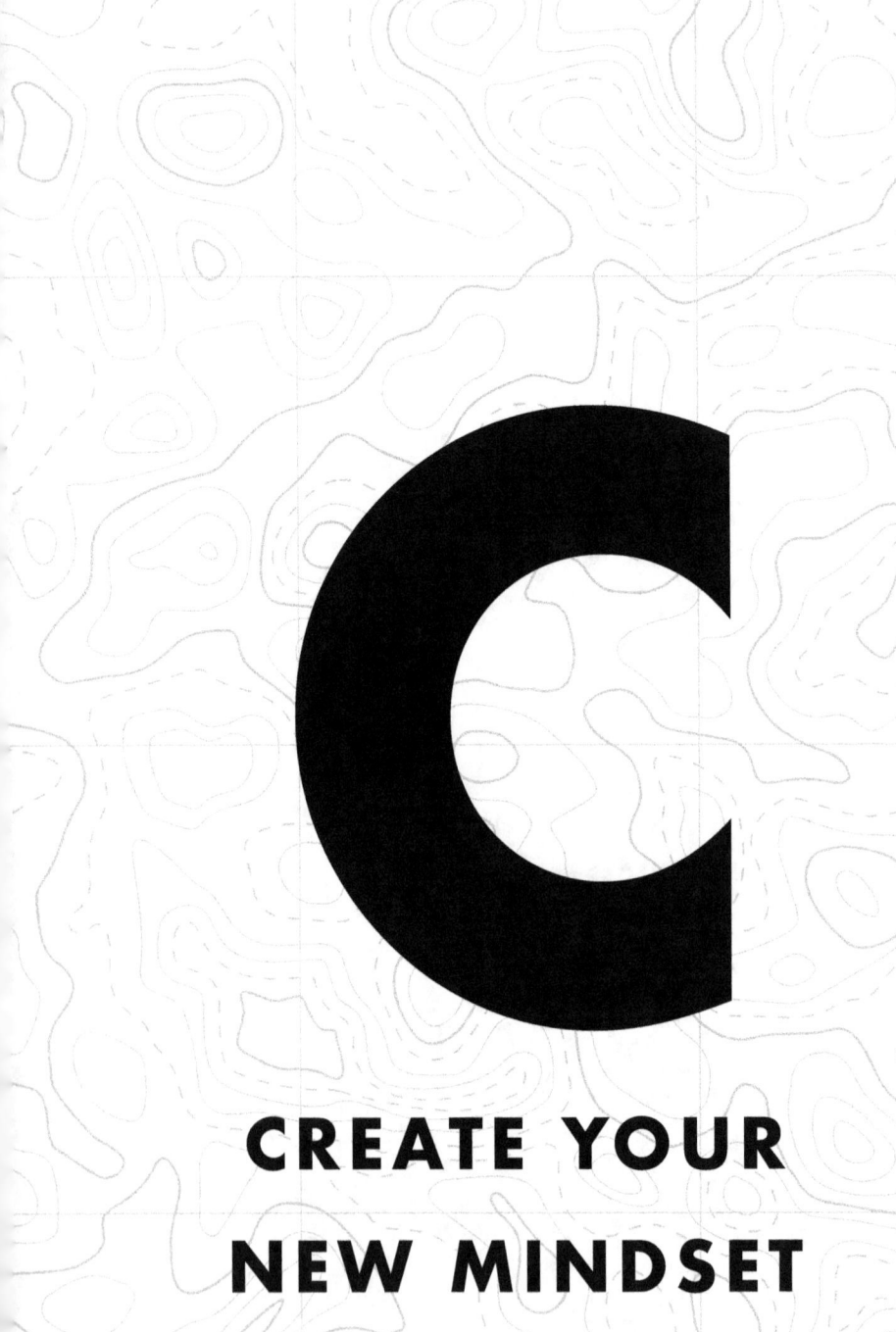

CREATE YOUR
NEW MINDSET

"We cannot solve our
problems with the same
thinking we used when we
created them."

– Albert Einstein

When you create a new mindset, you are originating an entirely new operating system for your life. Every mindset has its own unique code or language, and the mindset is created and reinforced through those very words. Your vocabulary and how you use those words to communicate to yourself and the world will either keep you where you are at, or it can be the missing piece that enables you to stop holding yourself back from so much of life. Your mindset is what has robbed you of your balance and joy in the day to day, but it is also what is going to get you back on track.

Balanced people speak, think, and act differently than those out of balance. Happy people speak, think, and act differently than sad people. Just getting by will have a different language than prosperity. People who love themselves unconditionally with agape will speak, think, and act differently than those who don't. Whatever you are trying to be will call for a unique way of communicating and thinking that is different from what you are doing now.

You need to align your mindset (which dictates how you speak, think, and act) with who you want to be. Continuing on your old path will only get you to where you don't want to be. Change your relationship with fear, anxiety, and other powerful but low-vibe mindsets, or they will give you exactly more of what you don't want. If you continue operating out of low-vibe mindsets like these, you will only reinforce your old thought patterns and reactions. You have the power to create a mindset that aligns with how you want to live, and operate moving forward for the rest of your life. It will take time to break out of the old patterns and mindsets, but you can do it!

Your new mindset will literally create new neural pathways, so be patient while that is happening. You are creating new ways of thinking—and that will require a little demolition and some construction. Your nervous system works hand-in-hand with your mindset, and neural pathways are reinforced through habit. The nervous system is responsible for how you react, and will need to adjust its reactions just as much as your mindset. Just be aware that your entire body will be reprogramming itself when you adjust your mindset and find your balance. So be kind to yourself during this transformation; it will be emotionally and physically exhausting at times.

EVERYTHING IS INTENTIONAL

Essentially, an intention is a plan that can be written, thought, or spoken. Everything must have a goal in order to have purpose; so every day, every second, in every situation, you need to have a goal or intention. Before every meal, every meeting, every conversation, every interaction, every text or email, set your intentions for the task at hand. Otherwise, you are a rudderless boat, and anywhere you go is from sheer luck. Without intentions, you are on autopilot. Without intentions, you cannot have plans or goals, only hopes and wishes.

Intentions are powerful tools, so be clear when you set them. In fact, every second you are setting intentions, whether you realize it or not. Every time you judge, criticize, etc., you are unconsciously setting intentions that you do not want to set. So it is not a matter of starting to work with intentions—it is a matter of shifting them so they work to your advantage instead of keeping you stuck exactly where you are at.

How you craft your intentions is crucial to their degree of effectiveness. Intentions need to be filled with high-vibe thoughts like gratefulness and inspiration (ideally, with little to no fear or anxiety).

You constantly reinforce your intentions through your language and communication. Create an intention with an affirmation, prayer, or mantra for every situation that you find yourself reacting to, and infuse those intentions with all of your heart. That is how you shift your old mindset and create a new way of looking and reacting to life. Don't just say an intention to go through the motions; say it with purpose and feel it. Repeat it, say it, think it, feel it, believe it! Your intentions are powerful, so instead of creating more chaos, learn to use them for good.

SEE IT FIRST IN YOUR MIND'S EYE

Visualization is the key! Imagine what you want in your life. Start with just a few minutes when you wake up and a few minutes when you are drifting off to sleep, and add more time as you are able. How do you want to live your live differently from this moment forward? Answer that, and then work backward from there. You need to be clear and concise in formulating your new mindset, so you need to be clear and concise with yourself about what that looks like. Before you tell yourself you don't have time for this, two important steps won't take but a few minutes out of your day.

1. For five minutes when you are falling asleep: focus on the good and don't give any energy to the bad. Reimagine the perfect day for yourself. Do not dwell on any negative from the current day. Or, imagine a perfect version of your life. No matter what you do, you must avoid dwelling on the negative or any low-vibe thoughts when falling asleep.

2. For five minutes when you wake up: visualizing how you intend the day to go is like placing your order for how you want your day to go. See it in your mind's eye

as if you are actually living and experiencing it.

3. Visualization is pointless and a complete waste of time unless you immerse yourself in it—don't confuse daydreaming for visualization. Visualization is purposeful and meaningful and has a specific structure that is aligned with the best version of yourself. Feel and believe what you are visualizing is true. Don't worry about how you will get there; just feel it as if it is your reality now. Then lock it in by setting your intentions. I can do this. I am worthy. Speak it out. Even yell it out. But just as important, you need to see it and feel it. See your visualization in your mind's eye and reinforce it with every aspect of your communication. Remember, who you want to be in the future speaks and acts differently than the current version of yourself. Your future self does not allow negative words into their mouth or mind, and your training to become that future self starts now.

AFFIRMATIONS FOR EVERY SITUATION

My personal affirmation practice started simply: I repeated them for 30 seconds, 3 times per day in the morning, mid-day, and evening. But it has evolved. I now affirm my intentions throughout the day, whenever my emotions and reactions trigger my realization that I need an affirmation to help jumpstart me out of any low spot, or any challenging or stressful situation. The following is my original affirmation that I still use to this day, with modifications as the situations require:

"With every breath I take, I call to me all persons, places, thoughts, and things of my highest path, power, and wisdom. With every exhale, I release from me all persons, places, thoughts, and things not of my highest path, power, and wisdom."

Setting intentions connected to something you do unconsciously, like breathing, puts your affirmations in overdrive, because you have now programmed yourself to perform those functions when you are not even consciously thinking about them. Intentions can be powerful, but their effectiveness is based on how you use them.

Try expanding your use of intentions by tying them to everyday functions you take for granted:

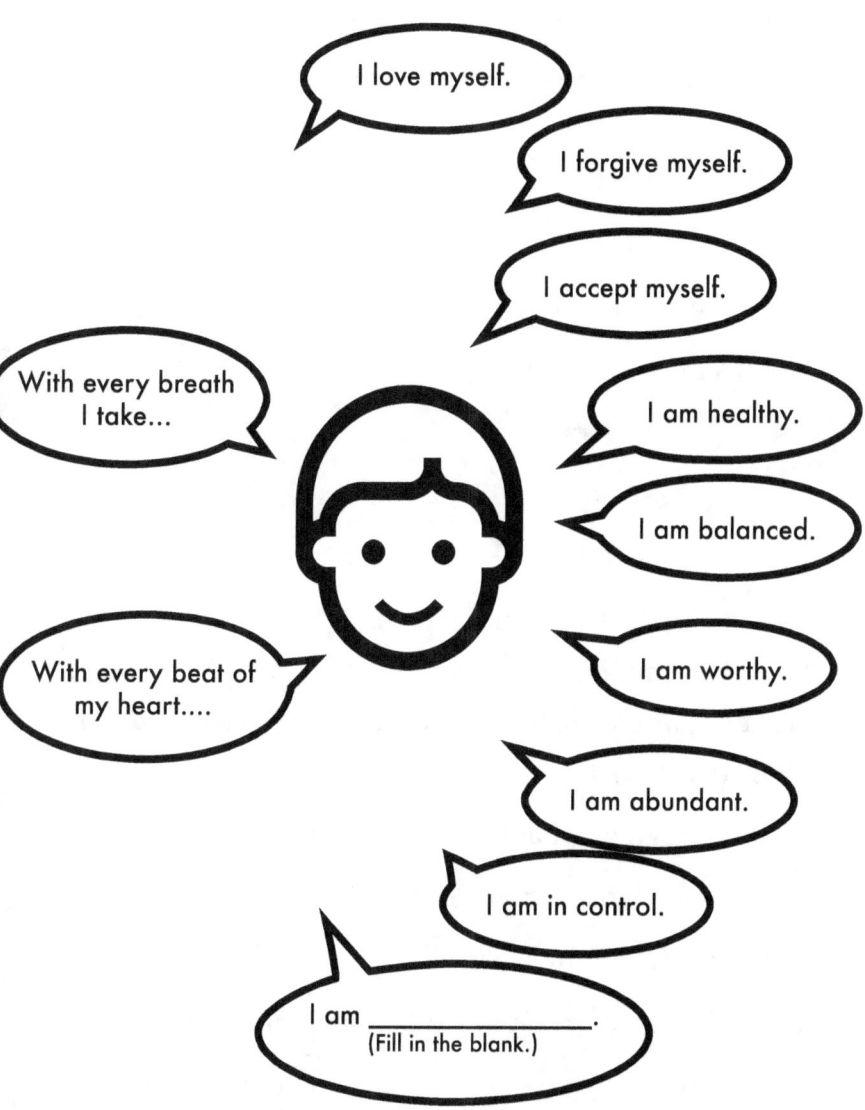

Use affirmations at times when you get nervous or need encouragement—turn your nervousness to knowingness:

"With every beat of my heart., I turn my fear into faith."

"With every beat of my heart., I can/will/do/am

_____."

(Fill in the blank.)

> I got this.
>
> I can do this.
>
> I am capable.
>
> I am unafraid.
>
> I am strong.
>
> I am loved.

You can also release and let go of persons, places, thoughts, emotions, and things (situations, circumstances, etc.) by again connecting an affirmation to your breath: *"With every exhale..."*

> I let go of what is holding me back.
>
> I break out of my old, limiting mindsets.
>
> I let go of my fears.
>
> I let go of past pain and disappointments.
>
> I release _____." (Fill in the blank.)

Remember, mindsets are mold-able. Portions of your

current mindsets are perfect and don't need adjusting. But there are parts that you hide even from yourself, which are doing the most damage. Moreover, many of your thoughts are limiting.

Any time you find your self-talk or internal monologue starts going negative, you need an injection of positive affirmations to help you jump-start out of any situation you are in and shift your mindset back to balance. As you uncover additional limiting aspects of your mindset, you need to create a new mindset, inch by inch and step by step. Creating a new mindset is putting the steps you have just learned into practice every day, every minute, every second. That is where your transformation really begins.

You should expect to continually evolve and strengthen your mindset for the rest of your life, as you shift through the different phases and break out of old patterns. Finding and maintaining balance is a lifelong process, but with the right mindset and tools, it will be possible.

YOUR SEASON OF CHANGE: 90 DAYS TO TRANSFORMATION

As you begin creating your new mindset, be patient with yourself. Even nature takes 90 days to transform from season to season. You can see and feel your own changes beginning almost immediately, but it takes time for the full metamorphosis. The first 30 days will feel the most challenging, the next 30 will get easier, and for the last 30 days, you will be sharpening your mindset and reinforcing your new habits. Keep in mind that it is impossible for transformation to not occur when you break out of old mindsets. This first stretch of 90 days is just the beginning of the shift that will occur in your life if you stay focused on your balance.

To create your new mindset, you need to take an inventory of who you are now. So grab your notes from the Break out of your old, limiting mindset chapter and continue to write down anything regarding who you are, how you operate, what triggers you, etc. Let's start with what has no place in your mindset—anything that is limiting or low-vibe: fear, doubt, blame, worry, disappointment, frustration, jealousy, unworthiness, judgment, or anything that makes you feel less than.

Next, make lists of who you want to be and how you want to live your life. Write out your new core principles and mindset for how you operate, in the present tense. What do you want your new mindset to be filled with? How about actions and thoughts that make you feel passion for life, empowerment, enthusiasm, belief, joy, happiness, or anything that ignites a spark within you. This is not the time to hold back and be timid. Speak your truth and truly make a decisions on who and what you want to become. Again, be sure to phrase your list with "I am," not "I hope to be" or "I want to be."

Whatever your list includes, see it every day, remind yourself of it every day, until it becomes a part of you. Write it down, copy it onto a sign, visualize it, think about it, become one with it. Align with it, feel it, then you will be it.

Act and talk like the person you want to become. State this in the now, not "in the future" or "I hope to" or "one day." Express positive thoughts of what you want, not negative thoughts of what you don't want. Observe your reactions. Try to learn and heal with acceptance and by adjusting your reactions.

Reprogramming your mindset is how you will rewire your brain and find your balance. That requires removing some aspects and adding some qualities. Think of it like this:

WHO YOU THINK YOU ARE NOW

KEEP
[GOOD]

REMOVE
[BAD]

ADD
[WHO YOU
WANT TO BE]

KEEP

Write a summary and/or list all the good stuff about you and your mindset. Include anything that makes you, you: positive traits, things you love about yourself, or characteristics that you want to keep.

_____

_____

_____

_____

_____

_____

_____

_____

_____

_____

_____

_____

_____

_____

_____

_____

_____

REMOVE

Starting with the limiting mindsets you highlighted earlier, write a summary and/or list what you intend to let go of or improve, possibly including thoughts, persons, places, situations, and any low-vibe activities or drains. Include all current aspects of yourself that are holding you back, which need to be removed or replaced. This list will grow as you uncover characteristics you have hidden even from yourself.

_____

_____

_____

_____

_____

_____

_____

_____

_____

_____

_____

_____

_____

_____

ADD

Describe the best version of yourself and your mindset. Write a summary and/or list the qualities and traits that come along with it. What other upgrades does your operating system need?

_____

_____

_____

_____

_____

_____

_____

_____

_____

_____

_____

_____

_____

_____

_____

_____

_____

NOW YOU HAVE TWO CHOICES:

1. Continue with the same mindset—and your life stays the same.

Or...

2. Devote all of your give a shit to how you want your life to be, and then construct your mindset around it. Speak, think, and act like the person you want to become. Using your affirmations to help jump-start your new mindset, reinforce what you want to become rather than what you want to eliminate.

The following is one of the most important contracts or promises that you will ever sign, but only do so when you are truly ready to transform and begin the journey to find your balance. Once you execute this contract, by signing it or simply acknowledging it in your mind, you are setting in motion the powerful wheels of intention that will help you create a new operating system and blueprint for living, to create balance in your mindset and shift how you view the world around you.

THE BALANCED
MINDSET CONTRACT

This is a promise to myself to take back control of my life and mindset.

I intend to prioritize my balance in all aspects of my life. My thoughts, whether spoken or not, have tremendous power, and I intend to be the best version of myself through mastering my mindset.

I resolve to remove what needs to be removed, to add what needs to be added, and to love and accept myself every step of the way.

There will be ups and downs, but my reactions and ability to focus on what I can control will keep me progressing on my journey.

I will no longer compare myself to others, and I will love myself unconditionally. I will no longer give away my power, allow others to disempower me, or allow myself to feel less than.

I intend to become the best version of myself.

I am in control of my life, thoughts, and mindset.

Signed _____

Date _____

E

EASIER THAN
YOU THINK

"You've always had the power, my dear, you just had to learn it for yourself."
– Glinda the Good Witch from The Wizard of Oz

Balance, transformation, or even simply seeing the good in life may seem hard at times. But living the rest of your life in a holding pattern, stuck in the prison of your own mindset, will feel like torture.

Stop writing the same story over and over—and start being the person you were meant to be. Seek and destroy limiting thoughts in your head and take back the time you waste on low-vibe drains. Simplify your approach to life and take out all the chaos that is derailing you from balance.

None of this will work until you reprogram your mindset, and bring consciousness and intention to everything you do, say, and think. Until you become aware and accountable for every thought and action, you will still be fumbling through life, blaming others and not living to your full potential. You need to no longer give power to the drains in your life. Nobody can break you out of the prison you have created, but now you have a few tools to help shift you back into balance and reprogram your operating system. You may need to shift a hundred times a day out of your previous thought patterns. Just keep shifting out of the low vibes and minimize the time you spend in the old mindset. Eventually, almost as if you forgot you ever had them, those unwanted, limiting aspects will no longer exist. You will now be operating with your new and improved mindset.

Are you focused on the right things or are you distracted? Do you dwell on who hurt or wronged you, or how aspects of your life are not fair? Maybe you have focused on creating wealth, but not on creating meaningful connection with your children or partner. If so, that can change the moment you allow it to. Maybe you have been focused more on the negative than the positive; that also changes the moment you allow it to.

The balance in your life is up to you, and it pertains not only to your actions, but to your thoughts and mindset as well. So every day you need to ask yourself: am I focused on the right things, or am I distracting myself with drains? Don't hide from that question just because you don't like the answer. Feeling that you could have done better is not an invitation to beat yourself up and continue the self-blame and sabotage cycle. Instead, it is an opportunity to first, observe the patterns in your life and operating system that are holding you back from the best version of yourself, and second, make the adjustments to shift into your best life. Evaluate everything you do and every thought you have. If any of these does not build you up, eliminate it from your mindset and instead, align with what does empower you.

Review the affirmations, prayers, or mantras you created to counter specific triggers in your life. State them the moment you feel any such triggers overtaking your mindset. If you don't, the negative, repetitive thoughts in your head will take over. It will take focused effort to break out of the patterns and habits you have constructed over the years, but that is the only way to take back control over your mindset and life.

Abraham Lincoln said, "Most folks are about as happy as they make up their minds to be." Yet few people actually embody that knowledge. Because they believe their own happiness is out of their control and is in the hands of others, when good does happen, they give that power away to circumstance or luck—but in reality, they created the source of their happiness. You have the same power and have had it all along, but perhaps nobody ever told you and empowered you to do so. Hear this: you have the power to create whatever you want in your life, whether that is happiness or sadness, joy or fear, balance or chaos. You just have to believe this and reclaim your power.

If you get frustrated, use your frustration as fuel. Frustration is a powerful energy, so are you going to use it for good or to keep you down? You are in control of how you use frustration or any other emotion.

Unsatisfied with any aspect of your life? Then use it as a motivator instead of a deflator. Use the power of any low-vibe thoughts—and jump-start their transformation with their own power. Turn fear into faith. Turn anxiety into trust. Flip every negative emotion to the opposite side of the emotional spectrum. This may seem impossible at first. But you can do it, and it will get easier every time you transform a low-vibe thought or feeling into a motivator.

Make finding and maintaining your balance a way of life. Prioritize this. Recognize when you are off-track and need to re-center. Finding your balance is not a destination—it's a journey. Change how you operate in life, and transformation has no choice but to occur. So focus all of your effort on what you want, and spend as little time and energy as possible on what you don't want. Setting an intention once or saying a prayer or affirmation one time does very little in shifting your world. Instead, you need to constantly speak about, think of, and visualize what you want. Nobody else is going to do it for you. So take control and empower yourself to prioritize your balance.

STOP BOTTLING
IT ALL UP

I learned a lot from television show Mr. Rogers'
Neighborhood. To me, the most important lesson was that
your "feelings are mentionable and manageable." What
that means is, you don't have to be afraid to talk about
what is going on in your head. Modern society needs to
break out of the mindset that "bottling it all up" is the
best option. Doing so only delays the inevitable. Do you
find yourself exploding or having a breakdown on a
regular basis? Everyone has their breaking point. So many
people are walking around pretending everything is fine.
Every day they swallow down all of their frustration and
anger and other chaotic emotions—and it all has to go
somewhere. By bottling up your feelings and not having
a safe outlet, you will continue to have breakdowns and
possibly hurt those around you.

You are in control and that is something you need to
remember. You are so used to your mindset that you can't
see it is in the driver's seat in every situation you are in.
It is that simple. Wake up! Stop living like a zombie. Be
conscious and observe everything you do, everything you
think, and everything you are feeling. Put zero thought

and energy into your fears or what you are trying to avoid. Instead, adjust your reactions and focus on the outcome you want.

DON'T QUIT RIGHT BEFORE THE FINISH LINE

Most folks quit on the verge of a breakthrough. When things are hardest, many times you are closer than you think to your goal. Quitting will just give you another excuse to sink into a low vibe and fill your head with all the negative things you have become addicted to telling yourself. You have to shift the mindset of quitting into a mindset of unwavering determination. Don't just do this for you—do it for your kids or other people that are in your circle of influence. Your demonstrating a mindset of determination can help others break out of the cycles and patterns that they need to remove, along with the mindset that quitting is OK when things get too tough.

There is nothing you do in life or even think that doesn't involve an even energetic exchange. Everything balances out one way or another, and you can't escape that. There is a cause and effect to everything you do. Don't run away from this fact, but embrace it. Live an empowered life. The way you want to live is not as far off as you think. You have been holding yourself back, and once you realize that, everything will fall into place.

Many have searched tirelessly to find out how to manifest

to get rich quick or to get happy or whatever they think is missing in their life. Here is the secret: you have been manifesting everything already! You don't need to learn how to manifest; instead, you need to take everything—thoughts, actions, reactions, emotions—much more seriously. If you can get off autopilot for more than a few minutes, you can start waking up to the fact that you do in fact create the day-to-day structure of your reality. Every thought, action, reaction, and emotion is part of that manifestation machine (even the thoughts you mistakenly assume you keep hidden from the world). Ignoring this is like ignoring your superpower. You have the ability to shift your life as easily as shifting where your mindset goes. Are you going to do that, or continue to give your power away?

I used to be an addict. I used to hate myself. I was on a path to an early death. Everything in my life has now flipped and the only thing that changed was my mindset. I would never have believed something as seemingly simple as my thoughts and mindset could change my life, but it did.

Life does not have to continue tomorrow the way it did today. No matter the situation in front of you, no matter the chaos around you, balance is possible. Never forget your power to find your balance and transform your reality. Your new life starts now!

I want to leave you with this…my favorite quote about transformation.

The butterfly said to the sun, "They can't stop talking about my transformation. I can only do it once in my lifetime. If only they knew they can do it at any time and in countless ways."

– Dodinsky